Arizona Cook Book

INDIAN

MEXICAN

WESTERN

ARIZONA PRODUCTS

BACKPACKING~CAMPING

PATIO~BARBECUE

A COLLECTION OF MORE THAN 350 AUTHENTIC ARIZONA RECIPES

Compiled by

Al Fischer & Mildred Fischer

GOLDEN
WEST ☼
PUBLISHERS

Foreword

We are wildly enthusiastic about eating... and we hope you are, too.

This cookbook came about because we'd been searching and searching for one just like it. For over twenty-five years, we've lived in Arizona, eaten Arizona dishes, and collected Arizona recipes.

Now we'd like to share these recipes with you... from the sizzling Indian fry bread to the icy cold gazpacho, from the tempting tostadas to the lighter-than-air sopaipillas, from the plump date pudding to the sturdy hiking bars, from the luscious sour orange marmalade to the aromatic barbecues. This book was created for lovers of tasty food.

As a bonus, ARIZONA COOK BOOK is a mini-guide to the people and products of Arizona. Standard recipes for Indian, Mexican, and Western cooking -- fry bread, stew, beans, chile, enchiladas, frijoles, tacos, tortillas, tostadas, sourdough, pinto beans, and beef are included. For variety, we've added variations of these standby recipes, plus quick-cooking versions for the modern cook.

If you like this book, better keep it tucked away. Better still, buy a copy for a friend.

Al and Mil

ISBN 13: 978-0-914846-00-0

ISBN 10: 0-914846-00-0

Printed in the United States of America

38th printing © 2007

Golden West Publishers
4113 N. Longview Ave.
Phoenix, AZ 85014, USA
(800) 658-5830

For free sample recipes for every Golden West cookbook, visit:
www.goldenwestpublishers.com

Contents

Indian Cooking

There are many different Indian tribes in the Southwest and their foods vary. Recipes are often handed down by word-of-mouth, and measurements are by the time-honored "handful" rather than by measuring spoon and cup. The recipes which follow have been contributed from long-time Arizona friends, as well as from the Bureau of Indian Affairs, the Office of Navajo Economic Opportunity, and the Navajo Tribal Museum.

Many of the fruits and vegetables we eat today were introduced through the Indians. Corn, potatoes, lima beans, squash, pumpkin, and tomatoes are the most commonly known of the plants which the Indian cultivated.

PIMA

Famous for their popovers and tortillas, this group accents beans and potatoes in their diet.

PAPAGO

Highly seasoned beans and fresh green chilis are typical foods preferred by the Papagos, who live along the Mexican border. The beans are often cooked with whole wheat kernels and cheese.

APACHE

Living in eastern Arizona, this group enjoys deer, cattle and fish in their diet.

NAVAJO

Staples of the Navajo diet are mutton, fried bread, and fried potatoes. Additionally, the Navajos harvest and roast pinon nuts, which are gathered in the late fall.

HOPI

Ground corn meal is an important part of Hopi religious services and culture. Their villages are located on three mesas in an area northeast of Flagstaff.

(NOTE: When making fried bread, be sure to put the hole in the middle, to allow the grease to bubble up and avoid a doughy center.)

NAVAJO FRIED BREAD #1

6 cups unsifted FLOUR
1 tablespoon SALT
2 tablespoons BAKING POWDER
½ cup instant non-fat dry MILK
2¾ cups lukewarm WATER (approx.
LARD or SHORTENING for frying

Combine flour, salt, baking powder and dry milk in a bowl. Add enough lukewarm water to make a soft dough. Knead thoroughly. Pinch off a ball of dough about the size of a large egg. Shape it round and flat with a small hole in the middle. Work it back and forth from one hand to the other to make it thinner and thinner. Stretch gradually to a diameter of about nine inches.

Heat fat at least an inch deep in a heavy iron skillet. Drop thin rounds of dough into hot fat and fry to a light brown on one side. Then turn and fry other side. As it fries, the bread puffs up and becomes light.

Drain each piece on paper towel. Serve hot with butter, jam, or honey. Makes about 18 to 24 pieces, about nine inches across.

NAVAJO FRIED BREAD #2

2 cups FLOUR
2 teaspoons BAKING POWDER
½ teaspoon SALT
½ cup POWDERED MILK
warm WATER (to form dough)

Mix flour, baking powder, salt and powdered milk. Add a little warm water to form dough. Knead dough until soft but not sticky. Let stand for two hours, covered with cloth, then shape or pat into 2-inch balls. Flatten into circle about 8 inches in diameter.

Fry in large black skillet, using an inch of hot shortening. To test degree of temperature of shortening drop a pinch of dough into hot skillet; if dough browns it is ready.

Fry dough until brown; then turn over and brown on other side. (Make dough very thin for a very crisp bread.)

NAVAJO FRIED BREAD #3

3 cups FLOUR
3 tablespoons LARD (or veg. shortening)
3 teaspoons BAKING POWDER
½ teaspoon SALT
¾ cup WATER

Measure dry ingredients into deep mixing bowl. Add lard and knead with hands until lard is in small pea size pieces. Add warm (not hot) water and knead with hands until dough is smooth and does not stick to sides of bowl. Knead at least 5 minutes. Cover with dish towel. Place in warm place and let rest for not less than 30 minutes.

Melt enough lard in a heavy 9" skillet so that there is about one inch liquid depth. Heat for deep fat frying. A small piece of dough when dropped in will rise immediately to surface.

Tear off a piece of dough about 2/3 of tennis ball. Pat and shape into a six to eight inch diameter and 1/4 inch thick. Poke a hole in center with finger. Drop into hot fat, turning only once so that each side is a light golden brown.

Serve warm. Sprinkle top with sugar, sugar and cinnamon, or powdered sugar, if desired.

INDIAN POPOVERS

3 cups FLOUR
2 teaspoons BAKING POWDER
1 tablespoon SHORTENING
Pinch of SALT

Work shortening into remaining ingredients as for biscuits. Add enough warm water or milk to mixture to handle dough easily. Work dough to a very smooth texture, but avoid the use of excess flour.

Form dough into smooth balls about the size of lemons. Brush with melted shortening. Let stand for 30 to 45 minutes. Pat each ball out with hands until dough is in a round, flat shape about five or six inches in diameter and about 1/4 inch thick, or a little thinner. Fry the dough in very hot deep fat. The dough should rise to the surface of the fat immediately. Cook until brown on one side; turn and brown other side. Do not prick the crust of the bread.

INDIAN FRY BREAD

4 tablespoons HONEY
3 tablespoons OIL
1 tablespoon SALT
2 cups HOT WATER
1 tablespoon (1 pkg.) active DRY YEAST
3 cups unbleached white FLOUR
2 teaspoons BAKING POWDER
2 to 4 cups additional FLOUR

(Start the dough mixture about 2 to 2 1/2 hours before serving.)

MIX together the honey, oil, salt. Stir in the hot water. Mix well. Sprinkle the yeast on top of mixture.

Cover with a cloth and allow to stand about 10 minutes or until yeast bubbles. Add flour and baking powder. Stir well.

Add more flour until mixture is firm and cleans the hands. Use from 2 to 4 cups flour for this step.

Place in a greased bowl. Turn over to grease top. Cover and allow to rise until double (about an hour). Punch down and divide first in half, then each half into 8 parts. Form each piece into a ball and permit to rise until ready to cook.

Heat deep fat to frying temperature. Take ball of dough and flatten with hands, using stretching action. When dough is very thin and about 6-8 inches in diameter, drop into hot fat and cook until golden (about 1 1/2 minutes each side). Drain on paper toweling and serve hot with honey or powdered sugar.

FRY BREAD

4 cups FLOUR
1 tablespoon BAKING POWDER
1 teaspoon SALT
2 tablespoons POWDERED MILK
1½ cups warm WATER

Put 4 cups flour into a bowl. Add 1 tablespoon baking powder and 1 teaspoon salt. Add 2 tablespoons powdered milk. Mix all together. Pour 1 1/2 cups warm water into bowl and mix with hand until soft. Take a ball of soft dough. Pat back and forth and pull until flat and round. Melt 1 cup lard in pan. Put dough into hot fat; turn until brown on both sides.

SQUAW BREAD

2 cups FLOUR
1 teaspoon SALT
2 teaspoons BAKING POWDER
½ cup POWDERED MILK
1 tablespoon SUGAR
1 cup warm WATER (approx.)

Combine dry ingredients in a bowl. Gradually add enough warm water to make soft dough. Divide dough in half and turn out on lightly floured surface. Pat into 8-inch circles about 1/2 inch thick. Cut into pie-shaped wedges. Slit center of each wedge. Fry quickly in deep hot fat (375 F) or in approximately two inches hot fat or oil. Drain on absorbent paper. While warm, dust with powdered sugar. (Dough that is overhandled will tend to make tough bread.)

KNEELDOWN BREAD

Corn is picked while still in the fresh, milky stage, shucked and the kernels scraped from the cob. They are ground on a metate until mush-like, and a little salt is added. The mixture is formed with the hands into cakes about 3 inches long, 2 inches wide, and an inch thick at the center. These are then covered with corn shucks which have been steeped in hot water until soft. The shucks are folded over the mixture with the narrow ends turned under, which gives the name of "Kneel down" bread (for this suggests a person kneeling).

To prepare pit: dig a pit about 2 feet square and 9 inches deep. A fire is made in the pit, and when it is thoroughly heated the fire is raked out. A layer of the prepared corn cakes is placed on the bottom of the pit, with succeeding layers over it, until all are used. Put wet corn husks or aluminum foil on top. Then replace with dirt and hot ashes. A small fire is built over all. Bake slowly until cooked, preferably overnight.

PAPAGO BEANS

Use small white beans for this recipe. Wash beans and soak for an hour. Simmer until tender, about 3-4 hours. For flavor variety, add meat or chopped onions.

SHAPE BLUE CORN BREAD

1 cup JUNIPER ASH
1 cup boiling WATER
3½ cups WATER
6 cups BLUE CORNMEAL

Mix 1 cup juniper ash and 1 cup boiling water. Put 3 1/2 cups water into a pot and boil. Strain the ashes into water. Stir. Add 6 cups blue cornmeal. Knead until a soft firm dough. Shape into small round patties. Put on hot skillet. Heat until brown on both sides.

MUTTON LOAF

2 cups diced cooked MUTTON
1½ cups CANNED TOMATOES
1 cup BREAD (chopped fine)
½ small ONION (chopped)
½ teaspoon SALT
1 tablespoon chopped CELERY
¼ teaspoon PEPPER

PUT the diced cooked mutton into a meat grinder and grind coarsely. Add tomatoes, bread, onion, salt, celery, and pepper. Mix well, form into loaf, put into loaf pan. Place in 400 F oven, 45 minutes.

INDIAN PINTO BEANS

2½ cups PINTO BEANS
7 cups WATER
1 cup BACON or HAM
1 ONION (diced)

Simmer beans, meat, water and onion together for 2 1/2 to 3 hours. (Do not permit to scorch.) Add salt after cooking. Serve as a vegetable.

PAPER BREAD

1 cup JUNIPER ASH
1 cup BOILING WATER
3 cups WATER
1 cup BLUE CORN MEAL

Mix 1 cup juniper ash with 1 cup boiling water. Put 3 cups water into pot. Boil. Strain the juniper ash into pot. Stir. Add 1 cup blue cornmeal. Stir. Let cool. Spread on a hot griddle or stove with palm of hand. Be sure the layer is very, very thin.

BLUE CORN BREAD (Loaf)

1 cup JUNIPER ASH
1 cup BOILING WATER
3½ cups WATER
6 cups BLUE CORN MEAL

MIX 1 cup juniper ash and 1 cup boiling water. Put 3 1/2 cups water in a pot and boil. Strain the ashes into pot. Stir. Add 6 cups blue cornmeal. Kneal until dough is soft and firm. Shape the mixture into two or three loaves. Bake in hot ashes for one hour. Brush off ashes and wash off. Serve warm.

BLUE CORN MASH

1 cup JUNIPER ASH
1 cup BOILING WATER
3 cups WATER
4 handfuls BLUE CORN MEAL

Mix 1 cup of juniper ash with 1 cup boiling water. Put 3 cups water into a pot. Boil. Then strain the ashes into water. Stir. Add 4 handfulls blue cornmeal. Stir. Boil for 30 minutes. Stir. Take off heat and stir. Serve cool with fry bread.

BLUE CORN TORTILLAS

2 cups BLUE CORNMEAL
1 teaspoon SALT
2 cups WATER

Pour salt into water and boil. Put cornmeal into bowl and pour the boiling water over meal gradually. Scrape the sides of the bowl until mixture makes a firm dough. Cool dough. Shape with hands into rounds, very thin. Bake on heated griddle until brown on both sides.

BACKBONE STEW

4 cups FRESH CORN
4 cups WATER
10 pieces BACKBONE of LAMB or MUTTON
2 teaspoons SALT

PUT 4 cups of fresh corn in 4 cups of water. Stir. Add 10 pieces backbone of lamb or mutton. Add 2 teaspoons salt. Put in a large pot and cook for one hour.

LIVER SAUSAGE

1 ground whole LIVER
1 ground HEART
1 ground LUNG
2 medium (raw) peeled, chopped POTATOES
½ chopped ONION
2 small chopped CELERY STALKS
2 tablespoons SALT
clean STOMACH

Mix one ground whole liver, heart, and lung. Add potatoes, onion, celery and salt. Mix well. Wash and clean stomach, inside and out. Put mixture in stomach; tie at top with a string. Put 2 1/2 cups of water into a pan. Cook sausage in water slowly for one hour.

BLOOD SAUSAGE

4 cups SHEEP BLOOD
1½ cups SHEEP FAT
1½ cups YELLOW CORNMEAL
1 tablespoon SALT
1 teaspoon red powdered CHILI
3 cups raw, peeled, chopped POTATOES
clean STOMACH

MIX 4 cups sheep blood in a bowl and 1 1/2 cups sheep fat. Add 1 1/2 cups yellow cornmeal and stir. Add 1 tablespoon salt and stir. Add chili and raw potatoes. Wash and clean stomach, inside and out. Put blood mixture into stomach and tie at top with a string. Boil for one hour in a pan with about three cups water in it.

ACORN STEW

2 pounds lean BEEF CHUNKS
1 cup ground ACORN MEAL
1 teaspoon SALT

Add water to cover beef chunks. Cook until tender. Be sure there is adequate water during cooking. Add salt. When meat is tender, separate the stock. Chop meat into small pieces to tenderize it. Add acorn meal to meat and mix thoroughly. Pour stock over mixture, stir thoroughly and serve hot.

MARBLES

1 cup JUNIPER ASH
1 cup boiling WATER
3½ cups WATER
6 cups BLUE CORNMEAL
3 cups WATER

Mix 1 cup juniper ash and 1 cup boiling water. Put 3 1/2 cups water in a pot. Boil. Strain the boiled ashes into boiling water. Add 6 cups blue cornmeal. Knead until the dough is soft and firm. Shape into thumb size pieces. Put 3 cups water in a big pot. Boil. Add dough pieces to boiling water. Stir. The dough will make its own gravy. Serve hot.

PIMA TORTILLAS

2 cups FLOUR
1 teaspoon BAKING POWDER
1 teaspoon SALT
½ cup LARD
¾ cup WATER

Mix together flour, salt and baking powder. Cut in lard, and add water sparingly, until soft dough forms. Flour board and roll out dough. Cut cakes six inches across and bake on lightly greased griddle. Turn frequently to brown on both sides.

NAVAJO TAMALE

4 cups SHEEP BLOOD
1½ cups SHEEP FAT
1 tablespoon SALT
4 cups fresh ground CORN
CORN HUSKS

MIX in a bowl the sheep blood and sheep fat. Add salt, stir; add corn and stir. Wrap up each in a corn husk like kneeldown bread. Bake in a low oven for one hour or boil for thirty minutes.

FRIED CHILI

Wash fresh green chilis. Leave the seeds in. Heat pork drippings and dip chilis into frypan. Turn chilis constantly until lightly browned on all sides. These may be eaten hot or cold. The chilis should be cooked only until they are crisped.

NAVAJO CAKE

6 cups WATER
4 cups precooked BLUE CORNMEAL
2 cups precooked YELLOW CORNMEAL
½ cup RAISINS
1 cup SPROUTED WHEAT
½ cup BROWN SUGAR

PUT 6 cups water in pan and boil. Add 4 cups precooked blue cornmeal. Add 2 cups precooked yellow cornmeal. Add 1/2 cup raisins. Add 1 cup wheat sprouted. Add 1/2 cup brown sugar. Blend well; dissolve all lumps. Pour into baking pan that is lined with foil. Cover with foil. Bake at 250 F for 4 hours. Cake must cook slowly.

GROUND CAKE

Grind browned corn very fine until like flour. Have water boiling. Add the meal a little at a time, stirring it until mushy with a Navajo corn-meal stick. Add sugar, which may be boiled into a syrup before pouring it in. (Raisins may be tossed onto surface before covering with corn husks.)

Dig a pit -- about a yard across and 10 inches deep -- and build a fire in it. When the pit is thoroughly heated, the ashes and embers are taken out, and the pit is lined with several layers of corn husks. The mush is then poured in. This must be done before the sun sets. The mush is covered with husks, then newspapers, and lastly the hot earth from the pit. A fire is built over this, which must be kept alive throughout the night. The fire must keep a steady heat to bake the cake. Just after sunrise the next morning the earth is removed, then the paper and husks. The cake is cut and served.

HOPI SPROUTS

Wash a container of bean sprouts thoroughly. Cover with water, add salt, and bring to a boil. Cook for 2-2 1/2 hours. Shell several ears of dried Hopi-corn. Wash them and boil separately. Cup up salt pork and fry. Add the cooked meat, drippings, corn and some corn liquid to boiled sprouts. Cook together an hour.

SMOKI CORN CAKES

(NOTE: This is a modern version of Indian Corn Cakes, created by the Smoki People (non-Indian) of Prescott.)

2½ cups CORN MEAL
6 teaspoonsful BAKING POWDER
¾ cup FLOUR
1 teaspoon SALT
1 or 2 EGGS
3 tablespoons melted SHORTENING
2½ cups MILK

Mix all ingredients until thoroughly blended. Fry on greased griddle, using lard or bacon fat as grease. Serve with powdered sugar or syrup. (Makes thirty-six cakes)

BAKED INDIAN PUDDING DESSERT

4 cups MILK
½ cup CORNMEAL
1 teaspoon SALT
¼ cup CORN SYRUP
½ cup SUGAR
½ teaspoon CINNAMON
2 tablespoons BUTTER

Put milk in a saucepan and add cornmeal and salt. Cook for 15 minutes and remove from heat. Add syrup and sugar. Stir in cinnamon and butter. Put into a greased baking dish and bake in 350 oven for 1 1/2 to 2 hours. Serve warm or cold.

Mexican Motif

Mexican cooking in Arizona is influenced by Sonora (the Mexican state immediately south of Arizona). The emphasis here is on wheat rather than corn; hence, the variety of flour-tortilla-type recipes. Mexican foods in other southwestern states, and in Mexico itself, will vary not only in flavor, but in terminology as well.

Ancient Aztec Indians provided the background for modern Mexican cooking, with their treatment of beans, chile and corn -- foods which are still the mainstay of Mexican cooking.

Visit a few of the local restaurants and start off with such basics as tortillas, tamales, tacos, and refried beans. Then, experiment in your own kitchen!

GLOSSARY

ALBONDIGAS--a rich soup in which meatballs are cooked.
ALMENDRADO--Mexican meringue pudding served with a custard sauce.
ASADA--spicy pot roast.

BURRITO--little burro.
BURRO--a tortilla folded around a bean filling.
CAFE con LECHE--coffee with milk.
CHILE--a variety of peppers, and the foods made using these peppers. They are the staple seasoning of Mexican cooking.
CHILES RELLENOS con QUESO--chiles stuffed with cheese, and dipped into egg batter and baked.

DULCITAS -- little cookies
EMPANADAS--pastry filled with meat or chile, baked or fried.
EMPANADITAS--little pastries.
ENCHILADA--corn tortilla with a filling, covered with chile sauce, topped with cheese.
ESTOFADO -- spicy stew.

FLAN -- baked custard with carmelized sugar.

FRIJOLES -- beans (generally pinto beans).

FRIJOLES REFRITOS -- refried beans. (Beans are cooked first, then mashed to a paste.)

GAZPACHO -- a cold vegetable soup.
GUACAMOLE--mashed avocado served as a dip or filling.

HUEVOS RANCHEROS --ranch style eggs with chile.

MENUDO--seasoned tripe dish.

SALSA--a dressing, relish, or sauce, made of chiles.
SOPAIPILLAS -- fried bread, generally served with honey.

TACOS -- corn tortillas fried and filled with ground beef, chopped lettuce, grated cheese.
TORTILLAS--pancake style of bread, made of corn or flour.
TOSTADAS--fried corn tortillas covered with beans, or chicken; also, small pieces of crispy fried corn tortillas.

GUACAMOLE #1

3 ripe AVOCADOS
3 tablespoons LIME JUICE
1½ teaspoons SALT
½ cup chopped ONION
1 can diced GREEN CHILIS
1 medium-sized TOMATO

Puree the avocados, lime juice and salt. Pour into bowl and add onion, chilis and tomato. Mix, cover and chill. Serve on a bed of lettuce. This mixture can also be used as a garnish for tacos or enchiladas.

GUACAMOLE #2

1 large peeled TOMATO
1 small ONION, chopped
2 cans GREEN CHILI, chopped
2 tablespoons VINEGAR or LEMON JUICE
 or LIME JUICE
2 peeled and mashed AVOCADOS.

Combine ingredients and serve with chips as a dip. May also be served on chopped greens with tomato wedges as a salad.

GUACAMOLE #3

1 medium AVOCADO
2 3-ounce packages CREAM CHEESE
2 teaspoons LIME JUICE
¼ teaspoon TABASCO
¼ teaspoon SALT
½ teaspoon WORCESTERSHIRE SAUCE

Cut avocados in half lengthwise. Remove pit. Peel skin from halves; mash pulp. Add remaining ingredients; beat with an electric beater until very smooth. Makes a creamy dip for crackers.

GUACAMOLE DIP

1 AVOCADO, ripe, peeled and diced
¼ cup MAYONNAISE   ¼ teaspoon TABASCO
2 tablespoons LEMON JUICE   SALT

Using a blender, mix all ingredients together until smooth. (Prepare this dish shortly before serving, since it will darken.)

GUACAMOLE DIP #2

2 medium AVOCADOS, ripe
1 tablespoon LEMON JUICE
2 medium TOMATOES, peeled, finely chopped
1 cup ONIONS, finely chopped
1 teaspoon SEASONED SALT
¼ teaspoon SEASONED PEPPER

Mash the peeled avocados with a fork. Add the lemon juice and blend. Add the remaining ingredients and combine thoroughly. Serve with chips.

GUACAMOLE DIP #3

1 large AVOCADO
1 medium-size TOMATO, peeled and finely chopped
2 teaspoons grated ONION
1 teaspoon LEMON JUICE
½ teaspoon SALT
1/8 teaspoon PEPPER
1/8 teaspoon GARLIC POWDER
1 cup dairy SOUR CREAM

Peel and remove pit from avocado. Mash with fork. In a bowl combine avocado, tomato, onion, lemon juice, salt, pepper and garlic powder. Stir in sour cream. Cover and chill.

GUACAMOLE SPREAD

2 ripe AVOCADOS
1 TOMATO, diced
2 tablespoons finely chopped ONIONS
2 tablespoons finely chopped PEPPER
1½ tablespoons wine VINEGAR
SALT and PEPPER

Prepare tomato, onion and pepper. Coarsely sieve avocados and combine all ingredients. Salt and pepper to taste. (Makes about 2 cups).

GUACAMOLE-CHICKEN TACOS

1½ cup GUACAMOLE DIP
1 cup cooked, cubed CHICKEN MEAT
Shredded LETTUCE
RADISH roses

Prepare Rosarita Taco Shells as directed, fill with guacamole, then chicken and shredded lettuce. Garnish with radish roses.

SALSA de CHILI (Green Chile Relish)

1 pound GREEN CHILE -- fresh, canned or frozen
1/4 cup VINEGAR   1/4 cup WATER
1/2 teaspoon SALT   2 tablespoonfuls CORN OIL

Wash chiles. Remove stems and seeds. Grind through a food chopper. Mix all ingredients in saucepan. Cook slowly for 20 minutes. Stir. Serve as cold relish.

SALSA #1

2 cups chopped, peeled TOMATOES
1 CELERY STALK, diced
1 ONION, diced
1 GREEN PEPPER, diced
1½ teaspoon SALT
1 tablespoon VINEGAR
1 tablespoon SUGAR
1 GREEN CHILE (or to taste), chopped

Combine tomatoes, celery, onion, green pepper, salt, vinegar, sugar and chile. Blend well. If a finer texture is desired, the salsa may be put thru food grinder, using fine blade. Cover tightly and chill overnight. Serve cold with meat dishes.

SALSA #2

1 No. 303 can TOMATOES (2 cups)
1 small can peeled and roasted CHILIS
2 medium ONIONS
2 cloves GARLIC
1 tablespoon CHILI POWDER
½ teaspoon SALT
Coarse black PEPPER
1 tablespoon white VINEGAR

Cut tomatoes into small pieces in a mixing bowl. Remove seeds from chili. Mix all ingredients together and cover. Leave overnight in refrigerator.

SALSA #3

2 canned GREEN CHILIS, seeded
4 medium TOMATOES, peeled and chopped
¼ cup GREEN ONIONS, sliced
1 teaspoon SALT

Using electric blender, whirl chilis, tomatoes, green onions and salt until very smooth. Cover and refrigerate.

SALSA #4

1 can (No.303) TOMATOES
1 can (small) GREEN CHILIS
1 ONION (medium)
2 tablespoons VINEGAR
2 tablespoons OIL

Grind tomatoes, onion and chilis, then add oil and vinegar, dash of salt and pepper. Cover and refrigerate for several hours.

SALSA #5

1 No. 303 can TOMATOES
1 small can GREEN CHILIS
2 ONIONS, chopped
2 cloves GARLIC
1 tablespoon CHILI POWDER
½ teaspoon SALT
1 tablespoon white VINEGAR

Cut tomatoes into small pieces. Seed and core the chiles and cut in small pieces. Add to the tomatoes, with crushed garlic cloves and onions. Add other ingredients and mix thoroughly. Cover and leave in refrigerator several hours.

GREEN CHILI SALSA

1 tablespoon OIL
1 chopped ONION
1 small can chopped GREEN CHILI

1 clove chopped GARLIC
2 cups whole TOMATOES
SALT

Heat oil, add onion, and simmer for three minutes in small saucepan. Add chili and simmer for an additional three minutes. Add garlic and tomatoes. Simmer five to ten minutes. Add salt and pepper to taste. Cover and chill.

BEEF TONGUE WITH SALSA

Cover a 3 to 4 pound beef tongue with water. Add a garlic bud and salt. Cover tightly and boil until tender (about three hours). Remove tongue from pot and dip into cold water. Slit outer skin and remove tongue from outer shell. Peel and slice thinly. Simmer cooked beef tongue slices in the "Green Chili Salsa."

GAZPACHO (Salad Soup)

3 cups TOMATO JUICE
¾ cup finely chopped CELERY
¾ cup finely chopped CUCUMBER
½ cup finely chopped ONION
¼ cup finely chopped GREEN PEPPER
2 tablespoons chopped PARSLEY
3 tablespoons wine VINEGAR
2 tablespoons OLIVE OIL
1 teaspoon SALT
¼ teaspoon PEPPER
½ teaspoon WORCESTERSHIRE SAUCE
Dash GARLIC SALT

Combine all ingredients in a glass bowl. Cover and chill for several hours.

GAZPACHO #1

6 peeled TOMATOES
1 seeded, chopped GREEN PEPPER
1 chopped ONION
1 chopped CUCUMBER
3 PARSLEY STALKS
3 cloves GARLIC
3 tablespoons OIL
2 tablespoons wine VINEGAR
1 teaspoon SALT
¼ cup WATER

In a blender, place the garlic, tomatoes, cucumber, green pepper and onion. When mixture is smooth, pour into glass pitcher or bowl and add remaining ingredients. Chill in refrigerator. May be served with ice cubes in each cup.

GAZPACHO #2

1 CUCUMBER, peeled
1 red or white ONION
1 peeled AVOCADO
½ teaspoon crumbled OREGANO
6 tablespoons OIL
4 tablespoons wine VINEGAR
8 cups TOMATO JUICE

Chop cucumber, onion and avocado into tiny pieces. Add oregano, oil, vinegar; pour tomato juice over mixture. Onion and cucumber slices may be added to mixture. Cover and refrigerate.

GAZPACHO #3

1 16-ounce can whole peeled TOMATOES
1 medium GREEN PEPPER, chopped
1 medium AVOCADO, cubed
½ CUCUMBER, sliced
1 2-ounce can PIMIENTOS, drained and chopped
2 tablespoons SALAD OIL
2 tablespoons wine VINEGAR
1 teaspoon SALT
1 teaspoon SUGAR
½ cup CROUTONS

Empty tomatoes and their liquid into a bowl. Cut tomatoes into bite-size pieces. Combine all ingredients, except croutons. Cover and chill well. Serve in small soup bowls; garnish with croutons.

FRIJOLES

½ pound PINTO BEANS
4 cups WATER
1 teaspoon SALT
1 teaspoon CHILI POWDER
¼ teaspoon crushed RED PEPPER
½ cup finely chopped ONION

Sort and wash beans. Add water, bring to a boil, cover tightly and cook 2 minutes. Remove from heat. Do not remove cover and let soak 1 hour. Add salt, chili powder, crushed red pepper and chopped onion. Bring to a boil, cover tightly, continue cooking slowly, stirring occasionally, for 1 1/2 to 2 hours or until beans are tender. Add more water, if needed, to keep beans from sticking. (Makes 3 cups)

REFRIED BEANS

2 1/3 cups cooked mashed BEANS
1/3 cup LARD

Heat the lard. Add the beans and cook, stirring occasionally until thoroughly heated. (Beans should be cooked very dry for frying purposes.)

FRIJOLES REFRITOS CON QUESO

1 tablespoon GREASE
1 tablespoon FLOUR
2 cups mashed BEANS
Grated CHEESE

To refry the beans: heat 1 tablespoon grease, brown 1 tablespoon flour in grease. Add 2 cups mashed beans, stir in and bring to simmer. Place in casserole dish, sprinkle with grated cheese, place in a very hot oven. Serve with broken fried tortillas.

FRIJOLES FRITOS

1 can (1 pound) red KIDNEY BEANS, drained
¼ cup (½ stick) BUTTER
¼ teaspoon GARLIC POWDER
¼ teaspoon CUMIN SEED, crushed
1 cup (4 ounces) shredded Cheddar CHEESE

Drain beans, reserving liquid. In a small skillet melt butter. Stir in beans and mash with a wooden spoon. Cook over medium-high heat about 5 minutes. Stir in garlic powder and cumin seed. Add reserved bean juice one tablespoonful at a time, to make the desired dipping consistency. Stir in cheese. Serve warm as a dip with chips.

HOT BEAN DIP

1 16-ounce can Rosarita REFRIED BEANS
1 cup canned TOMATOES, drained
½ can (4 ounce can) diced GREEN CHILI
½ pound grated CHEESE, Cheddar or Jack
¼ teaspoon ONION POWDER
¼ teaspoon SALT
¼ teaspoon GARLIC POWDER, optional

Mix together well in a skillet and heat until cheese melts, stirring occasionally. Serve warm as a dip with crisp Rosarita Corn Tortillas.

COLD BEAN DIP

1 16-ounce can Rosarita REFRIED BEANS
1 3-ounce package CREAM CHEESE
2 tablespoons grated ONION or ½ teaspoon ONION POWDER
1 teaspoon CHILI PEPPER
¼ teaspoon GARLIC POWDER
1 teaspoon SALT

Soften cream cheese. Blend in remaining ingredients. Mix well and chill. Serve with crisp Rosarita Corn Tortillas.

●

A word of caution when using CHILI POWDER -- too much will make a dish taste bitter. For each cup of red chile paste, mix one cup of red chile powder with enough water to form paste.

FLOUR TORTILLAS

4 cups sifted FLOUR
2 teaspoons SALT
½ cup LARD
1 cup warm WATER

Measure flour into mixing bowl. Sprinkle in salt and mix well. Cut in lard (or fat) with two knives, a pastry blender, or fingers. Add water slowly (mixing with fork or hands til ball of dough forms). Continue adding water til all flour is moistened.

Knead in bowl (or on floured board) til dough is smooth (about 5 minutes) and pliable enough to stretch. With greased hands, pinch off egg-sized balls of dough and set in bowl. Cover with cloth and let dough balls set from 15 minutes to half an hour. Shape dough balls into 6-inch circles by using rolling pin or patting with hand. (Flapping tortilla back and forth between hands helps keep it stretched.)

Heat ungreased griddle or frypan and brown tortilla on one side (about 20-30 seconds). When dough begins to bubble, turn and brown other side. (Makes about 18 tortillas)

CHEESE CRISP

Place a flour tortilla under the broiler until it is warm. Using a pastry brush, spread the tortilla with melted butter. Sprinkle generously with grated Longhorn cheese and return under broiler until the cheese melts.

For variation, add chopped onions and diced green chiles to grated cheese. Serve piping hot.

●

Flour tortillas may be purchased at grocery stores. They are often used as bread, directly from the bag, or heated over a GREASELESS griddle. Butter may be spread on them.

BURROS

Burros are flour tortillas wrapped around chile con carne or refried beans. To roll a burro, use a 12-inch or 18-inch tortilla laid out flat. Fill with chili or beans and roll towards you. Fold sides in toward middle and set seam down on plate.

GREEN CHILI BURROS

1½ pounds BEEF ROUND, ground or chopped fine
2 tablespoons FLOUR
1 tablespoon FAT
1 cup WATER
1/3 cup CHILE SAUCE
4 large FLOUR TORTILLAS

Heat fat, cook meat slowly and salt to taste. When meat is done, add flour and brown. Add chile sauce, then the water and simmer until thickened. Spread 1/4 of the mixture on each tortilla and roll up.

CHILI SAUCE

1 medium TOMATO
2 green CHILES, seeds removed
2 teaspoons FLOUR
2 tablespoons FAT

Toast tomato and chili and peel. Mash until very smooth. Heat fat and add flour. Add tomato and chile and cook, stirring constantly until thickened.

GREEN CHILI BURROS #1

1 ONION, chopped fine
2 tablespoons SHORTENING
2 cups leftover ROAST
  (save broth)
Pinch of OREGANO
Pinch of GARLIC SALT
Pinch of PEPPER
SALT to taste
½ cup FLOUR
4 cups BROTH or BOUILLON
2 cans roasted chopped
  GREEN CHILI

Saute onion in hot shortening until brown. Add meat and seasonings. Stir in flour and brown lightly. Then add broth slowly, stirring often. When gravy is thick, add green chilis and cook a bit longer. Fill tortillas with mixture and roll.

GREEN CHILI BURROS #2

Small BEEF ROAST, diced
1 medium ONION, chopped
2 small cans GREEN CHILIS
1 medium can TOMATOES, drained
CORNSTARCH or FLOUR
SALT and PEPPER to taste
1 clove GARLIC, diced

Brown diced meat in fat in a large, heavy sauce-pan. Add onion, green chilis (cut in quarters, with their juice), and drained tomatoes. Add enough water to cover, then add salt, pepper, garlic. Cook, covered, until meat is very tender. Then mix cornstarch or flour with small amount of water to form a thin paste and add to mixture to thicken slightly. Heat large flour tortillas on a griddle, fill with meat mixture and fold.

GREEN MIXED BURRITO

1 small can (4 ounce) diced GREEN CHILI
1 1-pound can TOMATOES
½ teaspoon GARLIC POWDER or GARLIC SALT
3 chopped green ONIONS
1 1-pound can ROAST BEEF (or leftover beef)
1 1-pound can Rosarita REFRIED BEANS
1 package Rosarita FLOUR TORTILLAS

Combine first 5 ingredients and cook slowly for about 30 minutes. Then add Rosarita Refried Beans and mix well and cook 10 to 20 minutes more.

Remove wrapping from flour tortillas and wrap in aluminum foil and heat in 400 degree oven for 10-15 minutes, until soft and pliable.

Place 1 to 2 tablespoons bean and meat mixture on one side of a flour tortilla and roll up in flute shape. Keep warm until ready to eat.

BURRITO ENCHILADA STYLE

Follow directions for Green Mixed Burrito, but fill and roll the Rosarita Flour Tortillas as for Enchiladas. Place in a shallow serving dish, pour over Rosarita Enchilada Sauce to cover and sprinkle with grated cheese. Heat in 425 degree oven 10-15 minutes, until sauce is hot and cheese melted.

GREEN CHILI

1 small POT ROAST (2 to 3 pounds)
1 small ONION
1 clove GARLIC
1 teaspoon OREGANO
1 teaspoon SALT
1 tablespoon FLOUR
¼ teaspoon PEPPER
1 can (14½ ounce) of TOMATOES
1 can (4 ounce) chopped GREEN CHILI

Cook pot roast until meat is tender and will shred easily. Remove meat, shred it and set it aside. Add finely chopped onion, garlic and spices to meat liquid and simmer for 10 minutes.

Make a flour and water paste, add to liquid and stir until thickened. Add tomatoes and chopped chilis, and the finely shredded pot roast. (If time permits, simmer the mixture a short while, being sure it does not get too thick.)

RED CHILI

The Green Chili recipe can be used for Red Chili, substituting 2 cans of tomato sauce for tomatoes and one tablespoon of red chili powder for the green chilis. Make a paste of the powder and water. (Go EASY on the red chili powder!)

GREEN CHILE CON CARNE

1 tablespoon SHORTENING
1 pound STEWING BEEF
2 pounds GREEN CHILE
2 - 3 cloves GARLIC

½ teaspoon SALT
1 teaspoon FLOUR
4 cups WATER or BROTH

Cube meat and brown in shortening by adding flour. Dice chile and garlic and add to meat. If hot mixture is wanted, do not remove seeds from green chiles. Add water or broth and simmer for an hour.

BEAN BURRITOS

Heat a can of refried beans and spread evenly on flour tortillas. Top with SHREDDED longhorn cheese. Roll tortillas into fairly tight roll, folding up one end to prevent dripping. Heat in 350 degree oven for 10 minutes and serve.

CORN TORTILLAS

While flour tortillas are served as bread, and are ideal for burros and burritos, corn tortillas generally are deep fried. They emerge as tostadas, as tacos, and as enchiladas.

2 pounds MASA HARINA
2 teaspoons SALT

Mix masa harina with water and salt. Shape the dough into walnut-sized pieces. Roll very thin and bake on hot, UNGREASED griddle. When tortillas begin to rise, turn over and heat a few seconds more.

OLIVE ALMOND ENCHILADAS

12 TORTILLAS
1 cup JACK CHEESE (shredded)
2 cups cooked PORK, BEEF, or CHICKEN
1 cup chopped ripe OLIVES
2 small chopped ONIONS
¼ cup blanched and chopped ALMONDS
1 can diced GREEN CHILIS
3 cans (8 ounce) TOMATO SAUCE
3 teaspoons CHILI POWDER
SALT
1 teaspoon OIL
Chopped GREEN ONIONS

Mix meat, olives, almonds, one onion, and salt to taste. Set aside. Heat oil. Add remaining onion and cook until tender but not browned. Add tomato sauce, chili powder and chiles. Simmer 10 minutes.

Heat tortillas separately in sauce until softened. Remove each tortilla from sauce. Place some of the meat mixture across the center and roll.

Arrange in a shallow baking dish, seam side down. Pour the remaining sauce over the top and sprinkle with half the cheese. Bake at 350 for 15 minutes.

Serve with shredded cheese and chopped green onion.

ENCHILADAS

To serve: cover hot fried tortilla with Mexican Cheese Sauce. Then add Chile Sauce. Repeat this process until three tortillas are stacked. Cover with Mexican Cheese Sauce and Chile Sauce. Then sprinkle with grated cheese. Place enchiladas in 325 oven until cheese melts. Serve on hot plate.

FRIED TORTILLAS

9 TORTILLAS
FAT for frying
½ cup grated CHEESE

Heat fat below smoking point in skillet. Fry the tortillas. Do not fry them too crisp or they will break. Drain on paper.

MEXICAN CHEESE SAUCE

2 tablespoonfuls BUTTER or MARGARINE
2 tablespoonfuls chopped BELL PEPPERS or GREEN CHILE
1 tablespoonful FLOUR
1 teaspoon SALT
1 teaspoon CHILI POWDER
1 teaspoon MUSTARD
1 cup COOKED CORN
1 cup TOMATO JUICE
1½ cups grated AMERICAN CHEESE
1 EGG

Melt butter in top of double boiler. Then brown the chopped pepper over direct heat in the fat. Add seasonings, flour, tomato juice, and corn. Stir constantly until smooth. Place over water and cook for five minutes. Add grated cheese. Allow it to melt slowly. Beat egg and add to the hot mixture.

CHILE SAUCE

2 tablespoons BUTTER
2 tablespoons CHILE POWDER (red ground)
½ cup ONIONS, finely chopped
1 teaspoon SALT
2 tablespoons FLOUR

Melt butter in a saucepan and fry onions lightly until golden. Add flour and blend well. Add chili powder, salt, and water, and cook until thick, stirring constantly.

CHEESE ENCHILADAS

12 corn TORTILLAS
1 ONION, chopped
½ pound grated CHEESE
(meat may be substituted)

Dip tortillas in and out of hot fat to soften; drain on paper towel. Dip tortillas in enchilada sauce. Place cheese and onion in center. Roll up and place in baking dish. Top with remaining sauce and grated cheese. Put in oven for about 15 minutes until cheese is melted.

ENCHILADA SAUCE

2 tablespoons FLOUR
1 tablespoon BUTTER
½ teaspoon GARLIC POWDER
1 can CHILI SAUCE
1 cup (approx.) WATER

Brown flour in butter, add chili sauce and bring to slow boil. Add garlic. Add water to thickness desired and simmer 5 minutes.

CHICKEN ENCHILADAS

1 can CREAM OF CHICKEN SOUP
½ can WATER
½ can diced GREEN CHILI
1 5-ounce jar BONED CHICKEN
¼ cup chopped ONION
1 small can chopped ripe OLIVES
1 cup grated CHEESE
12 Rosarita Corn TORTILLAS

Mix together soup, water and green chili and set aside. To soften tortillas, snap apart the corn tortillas if frozen and dip one at a time into oil that is heated to 350-400 degrees. Drain and stack the tortillas.

Mix chicken, onion and ripe olives together. Put a softened tortilla in a greased casserole. Put approx. two (2) tablespoons chicken mixture on center. Then sprinkle grated cheese and roll up. Continue until all tortillas are rolled. Pour the soup mixture over tops and sprinkle with rest of grated cheese. Put into pre-heated 350-400 degree oven for about 20-25 minutes.

CHICKEN ENCHILADAS with SOUR CREAM

12 TORTILLAS
2 cups cooked CHICKEN
1 pint SOUR CREAM
3 GREEN ONIONS, chopped
Shredded LETTUCE
½ pound grated Monterey Jack CHEESE
2 tablespoons chopped GREEN CHILIS

SAUCE for ENCHILADAS

2 cups TOMATO PUREE or SAUCE
2 cups WATER
4 teaspoons DRIED ONIONS
2 BOUILLON CUBES
1½ teaspoons SALT
1 teaspoon GARLIC POWDER
1 teaspoon OREGANO

Combine sauce ingredients and simmer about 5 minutes in pan large enough to hold a tortilla flat. Fry tortilla lightly in a little oil. Dip tortilla in sauce, remove and fill with cooked chicken or other filling, onions and lettuce. Roll up and put in casserole, seam down. Repeat until all tortillas are filled. Spoon additional sauce over top. Dollop with sour cream and cheese and heat in oven at 350 about 20 minutes. (Makes 6 servings).

(If tomato sauce is used, omit salt.)

ENCHILADAS, ACAPULCO STYLE

3 cups cubed, cooked, TURKEY or VEAL
1 cup chopped, ripe OLIVES
½ cup blanched and chopped ALMONDS
½ cup sliced, green OLIVES, salt
2 10-ounce cans Rosarita ENCHILADA SAUCE
1 cup grated PARMESAN CHEESE
12 Rosarita corn TORTILLAS

Mix meat with olives, almonds and salt. Heat sauce. Drop tortillas into sauce one at a time, permitting it to stay until soaked and heated. Place a generous amount of filling on each tortilla and roll. Arrange on large heat-proof platter, folded side down. Pour remaining sauce over them, sprinkle with half the cheese and place in hot oven for 10 minutes. Serve at once.

ENCHILADAS, American Style

        6 TORTILLAS, corn
        1/3 cup grated LONGHORN CHEESE
        ½ cup ONIONS, chopped
        1 tablespoon FAT
        1 cup CHILE CON CARNE

Heat fat, and dip tortillas in one by one. Take out immediately. Dip the tortillas in the chile con carne. Fill tortillas with one-half the onion and cheese. Roll into thirds. Put enchiladas into shallow pan with seam side down. Cover with rest of onion and cheese and bake in 375 oven until cheese melts. Spoon hot chile con carne over enchiladas.

TACOS

4 tablespoons FAT   1 TOMATO cut into half silces
½ clove GARLIC, mashed   ¼ head shredded LETTUCE
SALT and PEPPER   ½ teaspoon CUMINO SEED
½ pound GROUND BEEF   1 teaspoon VINEGAR
6 corn TORTILLAS (should be soft and fresh or they
  will break when folded)

Use two frypans for this recipe. In one, put 1/2 teaspoon fat and seasoned ground beef. Cook, making sure the meat is cooking evenly. Grind cumino seed and garlic together and add 1/3 cup water. Add to meat and let cook for five minutes or until dry.

In second frypan, melt the remaining shortening. Dip tortillas in hot fat until soft. Set soft shells upright into pan with opening at the top. Fill with meat. Heat remaining shortening and fry tortillas on each side until crisp.

Add a few grains of salt to the vinegar and 1/3 cup of water. Then sprinkle over the lettuce and tomatoes. Add the shredded lettuce and tomatoes to each taco and fill almost to the top. Sprinkle grated cheese over taco and serve with sauce.

TACO TREAT

Place one heaping tablespoon raw hamburger on flat, corn tortilla, pressing firm. Drop in hot fat. Cook about one minute or until meat loses pink color. Fold over to form a cup. Drain on paper towel.

To serve: fill cupped tortilla with grated cheese, chopped onion, shredded lettuce and chopped tomatoes.

OLIVE BEEF TACOS

1 pound GROUND BEEF
¾ cup ONION, chopped
1 clove GARLIC, minced
1 teaspoon SALT
2 cans GREEN CHILES
1 can pitted OLIVES

1 can TOMATO SAUCE
8 corn TORTILLAS
Shredded LETTUCE
Shredded CHEESE
Sliced AVOCADO
1 tablespoon OIL

Brown beef in tablespoon cooking oil. Add onion and garlic when meat is about half cooked. Add salt, chiles, coarsely chopped ripe olives and tomato sauce. Cook very slowly about 5 minutes. Meanwhile, fry tortillas lightly in oil. Fold in half, holding with fork to shape. Drain well. Fill tortilla with olive mixture. Add lettuce, cheese and avocado.

BEEF TACOS

1 pound HAMBURGER
1 ONION, diced
2 cups cooked POTATOES (mashed coarsely)
1 can TOMATO SAUCE
TORTILLAS
Grated CHEESE
Shredded LETTUCE
Chopped TOMATOES

Fry hamburger, set aside. Saute onion in hamburger drippings, draining off excess fat. Add one can tomato sauce, hamburger and potatoes. Mix.

Place 1 heaping tablespoon of mixture in center of corn tortilla. Press in place, drop in hot fat. Fold tortilla over to form cup. Cook until barely crisp. Drain on paper towel.

To serve: fill cupped tortilla with grated cheese, shredded lettuce and chopped tomatoes.

(Extra mixture may be refrigerated or frozen.)

HOT TACO SAUCE

2 small cans TOMATO PASTE
3 teaspoons CHILITIPINS
  (crushed dry red peppers)
¼ cup white VINEGAR

1 teaspoon SALT
1 teaspoon GARLIC POWDER
Pinch of OREGANO

Combine ingredients and mix. Add water as is needed. This recipe makes about one pint of hot sauce.

TOSTADAS

What is a tostada? Primarily, the tostada is a tortilla which has been dipped into hot lard, browned on both sides, and then covered with refried beans, chicken, or ground beef, as well as shredded lettuce and grated cheese. It's a type of open-face Mexican sandwich that lends itself to a variety of fillings.

REFRIED BEAN TOSTADAS

¼ cup LARD (heat in frypan for tortillas)
6 TORTILLAS
2 tablespoons LARD (for beans)
2 cups cooked mashed PINTO BEANS
¼ cup grated LONGHORN CHEESE
3 tablespoons shredded LETTUCE

Heat lard (about an inch deep) in a frypan. Using kitchen tongs, immerse individual tortillas into the heated lard. Turn tortilla to cook evenly, removing when light brown. Drain on paper towel.

While browning tortillas, heat cooked beans in lard in a second frypan.

Cover the browned tortillas with hot, mashed beans. Sprinkle shredded lettuce and grated cheese over the beans. (Serve at once, or tostada loses its crispness.)

CHICKEN TOPOPO (Tostada with Chicken)

12 TORTILLAS
½ cup OIL
2 cans (1-pound each) KIDNEY BEANS (drained)
¼ teaspoon GARLIC POWDER
SALT & PEPPER
4 cups leftover CHICKEN
2 AVOCADOS, peeled and sliced
1 cup LONGHORN CHEESE, grated
1 head LETTUCE, shredded
SALSA (see recipe)

Fry each tortilla in oil; drain on paper towel. Drain off all but two tablespoons oil. Add beans and garlic powder. Cook and mash until thick paste forms and beans are dry. Add salt and pepper. Spread bean mixture on tortillas. Top with chicken, avocado, cheese, lettuce and salsa.

CHILES RELLENOS CON QUESOS
(Chiles Stuffed with Cheese

8 fresh, frozen, or 2 cans GREEN CHILES (4 oz.)
1 pound Monterey (jack) CHEESE
4 EGGS
4 tablespoons BUTTER, MARGARINE or LARD
PARSLEY (garnish)

Peel fresh peppers by placing on an open flame until browned. Wrap chiles in a damp cloth to steam for five minutes. Pull peeling off.

Slit green chiles. Cut cheese into slices that will fit into the green chile slits. (Be sure to remove seeds and membrane.)

Prepare a batter by using one egg for every two chiles and one tablespoon of hot water to each egg, plus enough flour (1 tablespoon for each egg) to make a thin batter. Beat egg whites until they form soft peaks. Fold in beaten egg yolks and flour.

Drop the batter (the size of a 6-inch by 4-inch oval) onto a greased frypan. Place a stuffed chile on it and cover with batter. Cook over low heat until golden. Turn with spatula and brown on other side. Drain on paper towels. Place in baking dish, cover with sauce and top with grated cheese.

Heat in 325 oven until cheese melts (about 15 minutes).

SAUCE for CHILES RELLENOS

2 tablespoons LARD or FAT
2 ONIONS   1 can TOMATO PASTE (8 ounce)
3 cloves GARLIC   1/2 teaspoon OREGANO--crumbled
2 tablespoons FLOUR   1/2 cup WATER
                  1/2 teaspoon SALT

Heat chopped onions and garlic until golden brown in hot fat. Mix flour with fat. Add tomato paste, water, oregano, and salt. Cook to consistency of a gravy (about 15 minutes).

●

Chiles rellenos may be prepared ahead of the meal, cooked, and stored in the refrigerator. When ready to use, add the sauce and grated cheese. Place in 325 oven for 30 minutes (or until cheese melts.)

HUEVOS RANCHEROS (Mexican Eggs)

1 cup GREEN CHILI SALSA
4 oz. Longhorn CHEESE
4 corn TORTILLAS
4 EGGS
OIL and BUTTER for frying

Dip tortillas in heated oil and remove quickly. Set tortillas on baking pan to keep warm. In a frying pan, panfry eggs in butter until the whites are set but the yolks still soft. Put a fried egg on each tortilla. Heat salsa and spoon over each egg. Sprinkle grated cheese on top. Slip baking pan under broiler until cheese melts. (Variation: try adding heated refried beans on the tortillas, before topping with eggs, salsa, and cheese.)

CALABAZA CON QUESO (Squash with Cheese)

2 pounds fresh ZUCCHINI or SUMMER SQUASH
½ pound grated CHEESE
1 small can diced GREEN CHILI

Cut off stem ends and cut squash into small pieces. Boil squash until tender in salted water (about 15 minutes). Drain and put a layer of squash in a greased casserole. Sprinkle with 1/2 the green chili and 1/2 the cheese. Put the rest of the squash in and repeat, ending with.the cheese. Place in heated oven (400) until cheese melts and forms sauce. Serve warm.

MEXICAN SALAD

2 large green PEPPERS, cut into 1-inch chunks
1 medium ONION, cut into chunks
4 medium TOMATOES, peeled and cut into chunks
½ cup CELERY, chopped
4 slices BACON, fried crisp and crumbled
4 hard-cooked EGGS, sliced
½ teaspoon SALT
1 teaspoon CHILI POWDER
½ cup VINEGAR

Chop vegetables. Fry bacon until crisp; remove. Chop and add to vegetables. To bacon fat in skillet, add vinegar, salt and chili powder. Mix well and pour over vegetables. Serve on shredded lettuce.

ALBONDIGAS (Meatballs)

1 tablespoon OIL
1 chopped ONION
2 cans TOMATO SAUCE
1 cup WATER or BROTH
1 pound GROUND BEEF
SALT and PEPPER

½ pound GROUND PORK
1 slice crumbled BREAD
3 chopped green ONIONS
1 tablespoon chopped
  MINT LEAVES
1 raw EGG

SAUCE: cook onions in hot oil until wilted. Add tomato sauce, water or broth, salt and pepper. Cook on very low flame 15 minutes.

MEATBALLS: mix meat with crumbled bread, onions, mint leaves, egg, salt and pepper. Mix thoroughly and shape into tiny balls. Add meatballs to sauce. Cover and cook 40 minutes.

ALBONDIGAS SOUP (Meatball Soup)

Broth:
1 minced ONION
1 clove GARLIC, minced
2 tablespoons OIL
½ can TOMATO SAUCE
3 quarts BEEF STOCK
Sprig of MINT LEAVES

Albondigas:
¾ pound GROUND BEEF
¾ pound GROUND PORK
1/3 cup raw RICE
1½ teaspoon SALT
¼ teaspoon PEPPER
1 EGG slightly beaten

Wilt the minced onion and garlic in oil. Add the tomato sauce and beef stock and heat to boiling point. Mix meat with rice, egg, salt and pepper and shape into little balls. Drop into boiling broth. Cover tightly and cook about 30 minutes.

(Optional -- add sprig of mint about 10 minutes before soup is done.)

MENUDO A LA MEXICANA

5 pounds TRIPE (menudo)
2 CALVES FEET
3 tablespoons GARLIC POWDER

1 ONION (chopped fine)
3 cans WHITE HOMINY
SALT

Wash menudo and remove fat. Cut into bite-size. Split the calves feet and cut into small pieces. Put the menudo, calves feet and salt into a large pot. Cook over high flame until all juice is extracted. Lower flame to medium, and continue to cook until menudo is tender, but still firm. Add onion, garlic, and hominy. Serve with separate bowls of chopped onion and crushed chiles for seasoning.

TAMALES

1 pound CORN DOUGH (MASA)
1 cup LARD
1 pound BEEF ROUND
2 ounces CHILI POWDER
CORN HUSKS

Cover cleaned corn husks with water and let stand for several hours. Cook meat until tender and salt to taste. Shred meat, add pepper and cook to blend flavor. Mix masa with lard. Separate the corn husks into individual leaves. Spread masa on the center of leaf. Spread a layer of meat mixture on masa. Roll, tucking in the tip end of the corn husk. Lay in layers in a steamer and steam until done (about 40 minutes).

TAMALE PIE

½ cup OLIVE OIL	½ cup ripe OLIVES
1 ONION	2 CHILI PEPPERS
1 clove GARLIC	SALT, PEPPER and CAYENNE
1 GREEN PEPPER	1 cup grated CHEESE
1 pound ROUND STEAK	2 tablespoons CORN MEAL
¼ pound Ground PORK	1 teaspoon CHILI POWDER
1 can (No.2½) TOMATOES	1 cup CORN MEAL

MEAT MIXTURE: Shred green pepper and onion. Grate chili peppers. Grind steak. Cook onion and garlic in oil until onions are tender. Add shredded green pepper, steak and pork to onion mixture. Add tomatoes, olives, peppers and seasoning and cook for one hour, very slowly. When mixture is soft and mushy, add grated cheese, 2 tablespoons corn meal and 1 teaspoon chili powder. Stir in well and cook for a few minutes longer. Mixture should be consistency of baked hash.

CORN MEAL MUSH: Mix 1 cup of corn meal and 3 cups of water. Pour meat mixture into shallow pan and cover with the mush. Bake uncovered in 375 oven for about 30 minutes. Garnish with olives.

ESTOFADO

1½ pound STEW BEEF (lean)
1 ONION, chopped
1 clove GARLIC, chopped
¼ cup OIL
½ cup TOMATO SAUCE
1 cup WATER

3 tablespoons wine VINEGAR
1 teaspoon SALT
½ teaspoon PEPPER
½ teaspoon OREGANO
3 large CARROTS, cut up
3 large POTATOES, cut up

Put all ingredients (except for the carrots and potatoes) into 2-quart covered pan. Cover and simmer over low heat for 1 1/2-2 hours. Add the vegetables and continue simmering until meat is tender. (This stew will have a thin liquid.)

CARNE ASADA

4 to 5 pound POT ROAST
¼ cup OIL
1 chopped ONION
3 cloves GARLIC, pressed
½ cup SHERRY
SALT and PEPPER

Season meat with salt and pepper, then sear in hot oil. Add onions and garlic; cook until wilted. Sprinkle the meat with wine, turning the meat constantly. Add water, cover and cook very slowly. Repeat the wine-sprinkling until the sherry is used completely. Cook meat slowly for two hours, or until tender. Serve meat with salsa and tortillas.

MEXICAN SPOON BREAD

1 can (1-pound) cream-style CORN
1 cup CORN MEAL
1/3 cup SHORTENING (melted)
2 EGGS (beaten)
1 teaspoon SALT
½ teaspoon BAKING SODA
1 4-ounce can GREEN CHILIS (drained and chopped)
1½ cups shredded LONGHORN CHEESE

Combine first six ingredients; mix well. Pour half the batter into a greased 9x9x2-inch pan. Then sprinkle with chilis and half the cheese. Pour on remaining batter. Sprinkle with remaining cheese. Bake at 400 for 45 minutes. Cool 10 minutes before cutting into serving pieces. Accompany with salsa.

PESCADO CON FRUTAS (Seafoods with Fruits)

2 (1½ pounds each) LOBSTERS
¾ pound cooked CRAB MEAT
1 pound cooked SHRIMP
6 tablespoons BUTTER divided
3 tablespoons chopped yellow
   ONION

1 tablespoon FLOUR
½ pint heavy CREAM, scalded
1 CHILI PEPPER
1 cup RICE
2½ cups CHICKEN CONSOMME
18 ORANGE sections
12 GRAPEFRUIT sections

Cook lobsters in boiling water and remove meat from tail; cut in large chunks. Saute lobster meat, crabmeat and shrimp in 3 tablespoons of butter with onion. Sprinkle flour over seafood and add the hot cream. Simmer slowly with chili pepper for 10 minutes. Cook rice with remaining butter and consomme for 20 minutes.

Place rice in mounds on serving platter. Put seafood in center of platter. Arrange lobster claws around edge of platter, with fruit on top.

LENTEJAS con FRUTA (Lentils with fruit)

1 pound LENTILS
5 cups WATER
2 teaspoons SALT

2 tablespoons OIL
4 tablespoons ONION
1 clove GARLIC, minced

2 cans (8-ounce) TOMATO SAUCE
2 cooked or canned SWEET POTATOES
2 fresh PEARS, peeled and cored
2 large slices canned PINEAPPLE
1 large, firm BANANA, quite green
2 teaspoons MONOSODIUM GLUTAMATE

Add washed lentils and salt to cold or warm water in large heavy pot. Bring water to boiling point. Reduce heat and cover with tight-fitting lid. Simmer 30 minutes. DO NOT DRAIN. Slowly cook onions and garlic in oil until onions are clear and limp. Add tomato sauce. Cook a few minutes, then stir into the lentils.

Cut sweet potatoes, pears, pineapple into chunks. slice banana. Add to lentils and sauce along with monosodium glutamate. Simmer, covered, until the pears are tender (about 15 minutes). Stir carefully.

Dulces ...Sweets

EMPANADAS (Turnovers)   (Fried)

2 cups FLOUR
2 tablespoons SUGAR
2 teaspoons BAKING POWDER
1 teaspoon SALT

½ cup SHORTENING
1/3 cup ICE WATER
1 cup SUGAR
1 tablespoon CINNAMON

Sift flour, baking powder, sugar and salt into a bowl. Work the shortening into this as for pastry. Add ice water, using only enough to hold dough together. Divide dough into 12 even-size pieces. Roll out on floured board to make rounds about 3 to 4 inches in diameter. Place a spoonful of one of the following fillings on one-half of each round: thick applesauce flavored with cinnamon or any flavor jelly or jam. Fold the other half of the pastry over the filled half, wetting the edges and pressing firmly to seal in the filling. Fry in deep hot oil until golden brown and drain on paper towel.

These empanadas can also be baked in a 400 F oven for 15 to 20 minutes. While they are still hot, dip them in a mixture of 1 cup sugar and 1 tablespoon cinnamon. (Makes 12).

EMPANADAS   (Baked)

3 cups FLOUR
2 teaspoons BAKING POWDER
½ teaspoon SALT
½ cup SHORTENING
3 tablespoons SUGAR
½ cup MILK

Sift and mix the dry ingredients. Cut in shortening. Add milk to hold dough together and beat. Roll dough on slightly floured board into 1/8-inch thickness. Cut into rounds (makes about a dozen). Fill with chili, or taco meat, or with fruit mixture (apple, pumpkin, or mince). Use about one to two tablespoons of filling for each turnover. Moisten the dough edges with cold water. Fold empanada in half and seal edges together by pinching. Bake at 350 about 20 to 30 minutes. Sprinkle with confectioners sugar.

EMPANADITAS

2 cups FLOUR
½ teaspoon SALT
2/3 cups SHORTENING (solid type)
Ice WATER (enough to blend the pastry)

Make a rich pastry dough by combining ingredients. Chill dough for half an hour. Roll out and cut into small rounds. Place spoonful of grated cheese on one half of a round. Dampen the edges, fold over and press edges together. Bake at 375 for 20 minutes.

FLAN

1¾ cups SUGAR   2 cans EVAPORATED MILK
3 EGG WHITES   2 teaspoons VANILLA
8 EGG YOLKS

Melt one cup of the sugar over very low heat. Pour into a mold, tilting to make sure that melted sugar covers bottom and sides of the pan completely. Allow to cool.

Beat egg whites and yolks together. Add milk, the remaining sugar and the vanilla. Pour into the sugar-lined mold.

Place mold in a pan of water in the oven at 350 (about 1 1/4 hours), or until a knife inserted in the center comes out clean.

Cool a few minutes. Turn onto a plate while still warm. Refrigerate for several hours before serving.

MEXICAN CANDY

2 cups granulated SUGAR
¼ cup WATER
1 cup EVAPORATED MILK (do not dilute)
Pinch of SALT
2 teaspoons ORANGE PEEL, grated

Using a wooden spoon, stir a cup of sugar into frypan until caramelized. Add water. Stir until sugar dissolves. Add remaining sugar, milk, and salt. Place over low heat and stir until mixture boils. Cook, stirring until it reaches soft ball stage. Remove from heat. Cool to lukewarm, without stirring. Add orange peel. Beat until candy loses gloss and holds its shape when dropped from spoon. Pour into lightly buttered 8-inch square pan and cut when cool.

SOPAIPILLAS (Fried Bread)

4 cups FLOUR
1½ teaspoons SALT
1 teaspoon BAKING POWDER
1 tablespoon SHORTENING
1 tablespoon SUGAR
1 package YEAST

1 cup warm WATER (115--test with candy therm.)
1 cup scalded MILK

Dissolve yeast in warm water. Add to dry ingredients and the cooled, scalded milk. Mix well and knead dough 15-20 minutes. Set aside dough for 10-15 minutes. Roll dough 1/4 inch thick and cut in pieces 2x4 inches. Fry in hot fat. (More flour may be needed for smooth dough.) Serve with honey.

SOPAIPILLAS

1¾ cup sifted FLOUR
2 teaspoons BAKING POWDER
1 teaspoon SALT
2 tablespoons SHORTENING
2/3 cup cold WATER

Sift flour, baking powder and salt into a mixing bowl. Add shortening and cut in coarsely. Add water gradually. Mix just enough to hold together as for pie crust. Turn out on lightly floured board and knead gently until smooth. Cover and let dough rest for five minutes. Then roll out into a rectangle about 12 x 15 inches (dough should be very THIN -- about 1/16 to 1/8 inch thick). Cut into 3-inch squares or 2 x 3 inch oblongs. Drop a few squares at a time into deep, very hot oil. At first, turn squares over 3 or 4 times to make them puff evenly. Fry about 2 or 3 minutes on each side, or until golden brown.

Sopaipillas will puff up like little pillows. Serve hot as a bread with soup or guacamole. About 20.

MEXICAN CHOCOLATE COOLER

1¼ cups WATER
1 teaspoon SUGAR
1 teaspoon CINNAMON
2 quarts CHOCOLATE MILK

Combine 1/2 cup water, sugar and cinnamon. Boil one minute. Add remaining 3/4 cup water. Pour into 12-cup muffin pan and freeze. To serve: place cinnamon ice cubes in cups filled with chocolate milk.

ALMENDRADO

1½ envelopes GELATIN
½ cup COLD WATER
¼ cup BOILING WATER
6 EGG WHITES
½ cup SUGAR
½ teaspoon VANILLA
½ teaspoon ALMOND EXTRACT
Pinch SALT
RED and GREEN FOOD COLORING

Soak gelatin in cold water. Add boiling water to dissolve. Cool. Beat egg whites stiff, but not dry. Gradually add the sugar, alternating with the gelatin liquid, using an electric beater at high speed. Add vanilla, almond and salt. Be sure to whip thoroughly so the gelatin blends completely with the egg whites.

Divide the mixture into three parts, leaving one part white, delicately tinting the others red and green to resemble the Mexican flag. Alternate layers by spooning into a loaf pan lined with waxed paper which extends above the mixture. Chill at least 4 hours and serve with the following custard.

Custard   2 tablespoons CORNSTARCH
1 tablespoon COLD MILK
3 cups SCALDED MILK
½ cup SUGAR
Pinch of SALT
6 EGG YOLKS
½ teaspoon VANILLA
½ teaspoon ALMOND EXTRACT
Sliced, toasted ALMONDS

Dissolve cornstarch in cold milk, add to scalded milk, sugar and salt. Boil until slightly thickened, stirring constantly. Beat egg yolks, vanilla and almond extracts. Slowly add to hot mixture. Stir constantly until slightly thickened (about 1 minute). Chill. To serve: slice almendrado and top with the custard sauce and sliced toasted almonds.

CAFE CON LECHE (Coffee with Milk)

Make a very strong brew of coffee. Dilute it to taste with hot milk. Add sugar, if desired.

To use instant coffee, bring milk to boil and add coffee to desired strength.

DULCITAS (Little Sweets)

1 dozen Rosarita Corn TORTILLAS
½ cup POWDERED SUGAR (1/3 cup granulated sugar
   may be substituted)
2 teaspoons CINNAMON
½ teaspoon COCOA

Soften corn tortillas in heated oil, stack and cut into eighths. Mix sugar, cinnamon and cocoa in a small paper sack. Cook small pieces of tortilla in heated oil until crisp but not brown. Drain and dump into bag and shake in sugar mixture to coat.

BEAN SPICE CAKE

2 cups BISCUIT MIX	¾ cup MILK
1½ cup SUGAR	1½ cups Rosarita REFRIED BEANS
1 teaspoon CINNAMON	½ cups NUTS, chopped fine
1/3 cup soft SHORTENING	½ cup RAISINS (optional)
2 EGGS	¼ teaspoon SALT

Combine biscuit mix, sugar and cinnamon. Add shortening, eggs and 1/4 cup milk. Mix at medium speed until well blended. Add refried beans, remaining 1/2 cup milk, nuts, raisins and salt. Beat well by hand. Pour into greased pan 8x8x2; bake in preheated 350 oven for one hour (or til firm). Serve warm or let cool and frost.

Creamy Frosting

Add enough light cream to 1 1/2 cups powdered sugar to make a spreading consistency. Add dash of salt, 1/2 tsp. vanilla and 1/4 tsp cinnamon.

LITTLE MEXICAN WEDDING CAKES

1 cup BUTTER, softened
1 teaspoon VANILLA
1 cup POWDERED SUGAR
1 cup NUTS (chopped finely)
2 cups FLOUR

Frosting

1½ cups POWDERED SUGAR
½ cup BUTTER

Mix butter, sugar, and vanilla together. Then work in flour and nuts. Shape into little balls about the size of walnuts. Bake on ungreased baking pan about 30 minutes at 325. Do not overbake. Spread with frosting when cool and roll in coconut.

Western Ways

The southwest is synonymous with cowboys and prospectors, and cowboys and prospectors call to mind sourdough bread and pinto beans.

At round-up time, chuck wagon cooks would follow the cowboys with several weeks' supplies, including a substantial crock of sourdough starter. Today, there are as many recipes for sourdough as there are sourdough enthusiasts. Much of the fun of sourdough cookery, however, does come from experimentation. Basically, the starter is a combination of milk (or water) and flour which is exposed to yeast cells floating in the air. Given a gestation period, the cells start bubbling, and the process of fermentation has begun. One of the pleasantest ways to start an Arizona friendship is to share sourdough starter.

With sourdough bread and pinto beans, old-time prospectors could keep themselves fortified for weeks. "Pinto" is a Spanish word meaning "speckled" and, indeed, pinto beans do have dark speckles of brown on a creamy-white background. However, these brown dabs disappear during cooking, and the beans emerge as a reddish-brownish color.

In Arizona, pintos are commonly referred to as "frijoles," and frijoles, meat, and chiles are often combined into one dish. "Chile" itself refers to peppers grown in the southwest. Generally, the smaller the chile pods, the hotter the chile.

Sourdough

SOURDOUGH STARTER #1

1 cup MILK
1 cup FLOUR

To begin, place one cup milk in a glass jar or crock (nothing metal) and allow to stand at room temperature for 24 hours.

Stir in 1 cup flour. (To speed the process, cover jar with cheesecloth and place outside for several hours to expose dough to the wild yeast cells floating in the wind.)

Leave uncovered in a warm place (80 is ideal) for 2 to 5 days, depending on how long it takes to bubble and sour. (May be kept near the pilot light on a gas range.) If it starts to dry out, stir in enough moderately warm water to bring it back to the original consistency. Once it has a good sour aroma and is full of bubbles, it is ready to use.

This starter is best if you use it at least once a week. If it is not used for two or three weeks, spoon out and discard about half of the starter and replenish it as described above. If you don't plan to use the starter for several weeks or more it is a good idea to freeze it. Since freezing slows down the yeast action, leave it at room temperature for 24 hours after thawing.

Each time you use part of your starter, replenish it with a mixture of equal amounts of milk and flour. Leave at room temperature for several hours until it becomes full of bubbles. Then cover and store it in the refrigerator.

SOURDOUGH STARTER #2

1 cake YEAST dissolved in 2 cups warm WATER
Add 2 cups FLOUR and place in crockery or
pottery bowl (NOT in metal)
Let set in warm place for 3 or 4 days.

When it begins to ferment, skim off top. This scum will be quite thick and may have to be skimmed way down. Add enough flour and water to make a consistency of paste. To keep alive, add flour and water same as above and skim off as it works.

SOURDOUGH POT

Take a gallon crock or wooden bucket and put in the following:

2 cups **FLOUR**
1 teaspoon **SALT**
3 tablespoons **SUGAR**
½ teaspoon **DRY YEAST**
2 cups lukewarm **WATER**

Stir mixture until a smooth thin paste. Put on lid and set in a warm place to sour. Stir it several times a day. In two or three days the sourdough will be ready.

If no yeast is available, add 4 tablespoons sugar and 1 1/2 teaspoons salt to the starter and it will sour, too, except the process will take about 5 days.

To keep starter active, add one cup unsifted flour and one cup warm water and let stand at room temperature either all night or all day. Do this at least once a week. Always reserve one-half cup or more of starter and store in refrigerator.

SOURDOUGH PANCAKES #1

½ cup **SOURDOUGH STARTER**
2 cups **FLOUR**
2 cups lukewarm **WATER**
2 level tablespoons **SUGAR**
1 teaspoon **SALT**
3 tablespoons melted **SHORTENING or OIL**
2 **EGGS**
1 teaspoon **BAKING SODA**

To the 1/2 cup of starter add 2 cups of flour and two cups lukewarm water. Beat until smooth and let stand in a warm place overnight.

To the hotcake dough, add sugar, salt and melted shortening or oil. Beat in eggs. Dissolve soda in one tablespoon water and fold in gently. Do not stir after soda has been added. Grease griddle and bake.

SOURDOUGH BUCKWHEATS

Follow pancake recipe, but in place of the flour called for, substitute 1 1/2 cups buckwheat flour and 1/4 to 1/2 cup white flour.

SOURDOUGH PANCAKES #2

½ cup SOURDOUGH STARTER
1 cup undiluted EVAPORATED MILK
1 cup warm WATER
1¾ to 2 cups unsifted FLOUR
2 EGGS
2 tablespoons SUGAR
½ teaspoon SALT
About 1 teaspoon SODA

Combine starter, evaporated milk, water, and flour in a large bowl; mix to blend and leave at room temperature overnight. The next morning, add eggs, sugar and salt and soda and mix well (don't beat!). Cook on a greased griddle over moderate heat. Do not let griddle smoke! Turn when top side is full of broken bubbles and has lost glossiness. Makes 30 dollar-size or a dozen 6-inch pancakes.

SOURDOUGH BISCUITS

½ cup SOURDOUGH STARTER
1 cup milk
2½ cups unsifted FLOUR
¾ teaspoon SALT
1 tablespoon SUGAR
1 teaspoon double-acting BAKING POWDER
About ½ teaspoon SODA
SALAD OIL or BUTTER or BACON GREASE

Mix the starter, milk and 1 cup of the flour in a large bowl. (Prepare this the night before for breakfast.) Cover the bowl and keep at room temperature to let rise.

Turn this very soft dough out onto 1 cup flour on a bread board. Combine salt, sugar, baking powder, and soda with remaining 1/2 cup flour and sift over the top. With your hands, mix dry ingredients into the soft dough, kneading lightly to get correct consistency. Roll out to a 1/2 inch thickness. Cut out biscuits with a cutter and dip each in either warm bacon grease OR a mixture of half salad oil and half melted butter.

Place close together in a 9 1/2 inch square pan and set in a warm place to let rise for about 1/2 hour. Bake in a moderately hot oven (375 F) for half an hour. (Makes about 14 biscuits.)

HAYDEN SOURDOUGH BREAD

1 package active dry YEAST
1½ cups warm WATER
1 cup SOURDOUGH STARTER BATTER
2 teaspoons SUGAR
1½ teaspoons SALT
5 cups sifted Family Kitchen or Rose FLOUR
½ teaspoon BAKING SODA

In large mixing bowl, soften yeast in the warm water. Blend in starter batter, sugar, and salt. Add 3 1/2 cups flour. Beat 3 or 4 minutes. Cover and let rise in a warm place until double, about 1 1/2 hours. Mix baking soda with remaining 1 1/2 cups flour. Stir into dough. Add enough additional flour, about 1/2 cup, to make a stiff dough. Turn out on lightly floured surface and knead 8 to 10 minutes.

Shape into 1 large or 2 medium loaves. Place on lightly greased baking sheets. Let rise in warm place until double, about 1 1/2 hours. Bake in 400 oven for 35 to 40 minutes for medium loaves and 40 to 45 minutes for large loaf.

To shape Round Loaves

Form into ball shape and place on baking sheet. Slightly flatten top with hand and make vertical cuts about 1/4" deep around each loaf at 2-inch intervals with a sharp knife.

To shape French Bread

Divide dough in half. Roll each half into 15x10" oblong. Beginning with wide side, roll up tightly toward you. Seal edges by pinching together. Roll back and forth to lengthen loaf and taper ends. Place diagonally on lightly-greased corn-meal-sprinkled baking sheet. Make 1/4" slashes in dough at 2" intervals.

SOURDOUGH BREAD STICKS

Make dough as directed,but shape into 2 balls. Roll each ball out on floured board to 1/2" thick. Slice dough in long strips, 1/2" wide and roll each strip with your hands on floured board to make them cylindrical. Brush with water and place about 1" apart on lightly greased baking sheet. Let rise in warm place for 30 minutes and bake at 400 for 20 minutes.

SOURDOUGH DATE LOAF

½ cup **SOURDOUGH STARTER**
1½ cups unsifted **FLOUR**
1 cup undiluted **EVAPORATED MILK**
2 tablespoons **SUGAR**
¼ cup **BUTTER** or **MARGARINE**
¾ cup **BROWN SUGAR**
1 cup chopped **DATES**
½ cup chopped **WALNUTS**
2 beaten **EGGS**
½ cup quick-cooking **ROLLED OATS**
1 teaspoon **BAKING POWDER**
½ teaspoon **EACH** of **SODA** and **SALT**

The night before, combine starter, flour, undiluted evaporated milk, and sugar; partially cover and leave at room temperature overnight. Next day, cream butter and brown sugar. Add dates and nuts; set aside. Combine eggs, rolled oats, baking powder, soda, and salt; stir into the sourdough mixture with date mixture. Turn into greased loaf pan (5 x 9 in.) and let rise about 1 hour. Bake in a moderately hot oven (375 F) for one hour. Cool for 10 minutes in pan, then remove from pan to cooling rack. Serve warm or cool. Makes one loaf.

SOURDOUGH BREAD

1 quart **SOURDOUGH**
1 quart lukewarm **WATER**
¾ cup or 1 cup **SUGAR**
2 tablespoons **SALT**
6 tablespoons melted **SHORTENING**
12 cups **FLOUR**

Mix ingredients in the order given, adding flour last, using enough to make a dough that can be handled. Knead until smooth and elastic. Place in a greased bowl and let rise. It will take longer than yeast bread. Knead it down and let it rise again.

Shape into four oblong loaves and place on a lightly greased cooky sheet. Cover and set in warm place. Let rise to nearly double in size. Just before baking, brush outside with water; make diagonal slashes across the top with a sharp knife. Bake in a 350 F oven for an hour.

SOURDOUGH BREAD (Short Method)

1½ cups warm WATER
1 package YEAST (active dry or compressed)
1 cup SOURDOUGH STARTER
4 cups unsifted FLOUR
2 teaspoons EACH SUGAR and SALT
About ½ teaspoon SODA
About 2 cups unsifted FLOUR

Pour warm water into a large mixing bowl. Stir in the yeast. Add starter, the 4 cups flour, salt and sugar. Stir vigorously for about 3 minutes with a wooden spoon. Turn into a large greased bowl. Cover with a towel and let rise in a warm place until double in bulk (1 1/2 to 2 hours). Mix soda with 1 cup of the remaining flour and stir in; the dough will be very stiff. Turn dough out onto a floured board and begin kneading. Add the remaining 1 cup flour (or more) to control the stickiness. Knead until satiny -- about 5 to 8 minutes.

Shape into two oblong loaves or one large round loaf. Place on a lightly greased cooky sheet. Cover. Place in a warm place. Let rise to nearly double in size (about 1 to 1 1/2 hours). Just before baking, brush outside with water; make diagonal slashes across the top with a sharp knife.

Put a shallow pan of hot water in the bottom of the oven. Bake in a hot oven (400 F) until the crust is a medium dark brown (about 45 minutes for oblong loaves and about 50 minutes for the round loaf.)

SOURDOUGH MUFFINS

½ cup WHOLE WHEAT FLOUR
1½ cups WHITE FLOUR
½ cup melted SHORTENING
½ cup SUGAR
½ cup EVAPORATED MILK (do not dilute)
2 EGGS
1 cup RAISINS
1 teaspoon SALT
1 teaspoon SODA
½ cup SOURDOUGH

Stir only enough to blend. Bake in greased muffin pans at 425 for 25 minutes. In place of the canned milk 1/2 cup water plus two tablespoons dry milk can be substituted.

SOURDOUGH BREAD (Long Method)

(This recipe takes 24 hours from start to finish. The bread is denser in texture than the loaf made with commercial yeast.)

1½ cups warm WATER
1 cup SOURDOUGH STARTER
4 cups unsifted FLOUR
2 teaspoons EACH of SUGAR and SALT
2 cups unsifted FLOUR (more or less)
½ teaspoon SODA (or more)

Combine water, starter, 4 cups flour, salt and sugar. Mix well, place in a crock and leave at room temperature about 18 hours or until the sponge has doubled in size. Stir in 1 cup of the remaining flour which has been mixed with the soda. The resulting dough will be very stiff. Turn dough out onto a floured board and knead, adding remaining 1 cup flour as needed. Knead until smooth -- 5 to 8 minutes.

Shape into two oblong loaves or one large round loaf. Place on a lightly greased cooky sheet. Cover and place in a warm place for 3 to 4 hours, or until nearly double in size. Just before baking, brush with water. Make diagonal slits in the top with a sharp knife. Place a shallow pan of hot water in the bottom of the oven. Bake in a hot oven (400 F) until crust is a medium dark brown (about 45 minutes for the oblong loaves, 50 minutes for the large round loaf).

SOURDOUGH CORN BREAD

1 cup SOURDOUGH STARTER
1½ cups YELLOW CORNMEAL
1½ cups EVAPORATED MILK
2 EGGS, beaten
2 tablespoons SUGAR
¼ cup melted BUTTER (warm)
½ teaspoon SALT
About ¾ teaspoon SODA

Thoroughly mix the starter, cornmeal, evaporated milk, eggs, and sugar in a large bowl. Stir in melted butter, salt and soda. Turn into 10-inch greased pan and bake in hot oven (450 F) for 30 minutes. Serve hot.

GREER NEAL'S SOURDOUGH ENGLISH MUFFINS

½ cup STARTER
1 cup MILK
2¾ cups FLOUR
1 tablespoon SUGAR
¾ teaspoon SALT
½ teaspoon SODA
CORNMEAL

In a large mixing bowl, combine starter, milk and two cups flour. Mix together, cover and set at room temperature about eight hours (or overnight). Mix 1/2 cup flour, sugar, salt and soda; sprinkle over dough; mix in thoroughly. Turn this very stiff dough out onto a board floured with remaining 1/4-cup flour. Knead about two or three minutes.

Roll out to 3/4-inch thickness. Use a 3-inch cutter or tuna can with ends removed to cut nine muffins. Place one-inch apart on cookie sheet. Cover with towel and let rise an hour. Sprinkle both sides with corn meal and bake at 300 degrees in lightly greased electric frypan with cover on for 10 minutes on each side. Split and serve hot with butter and honey or jam.

GREER NEAL'S SOURDOUGH DROP COOKIES

½ cup STARTER
1 cup undiluted CANNED MILK
2 cups FLOUR
1 cup BUTTER or MARGARINE
1¼ cups DARK BROWN SUGAR
1 beaten EGG
½ teaspoon EACH--SALT & SODA
3 cups CORN FLAKES, crushed
¾ cup chopped WALNUTS
¾ cup shredded COCONUT (optional)

Stir starter, milk and 1 1/2 cups flour together in a large bowl. Set aside for two hours. Meanwhile, cream sugar and butter; blend in egg and a mixture of 1/2 cup flour, salt and soda. Stir in corn flakes, walnuts and coconut. Blend both mixtures together. Drop batter from a teaspoon onto greased cookie sheet, placing mounds two inches apart. Bake 15 minutes at 375 degrees. (Makes 60).

SALT RIVER SOURDOUGH STARTER

1 package active dry YEAST
½ cup warm WATER
2 cups sifted Family Kitchen or Rose FLOUR
2 cups lukewarm WATER
1 tablespoon SUGAR
1 teaspoon SALT

In a large mixing bowl, dissolve the yeast in warm water.   Stir in flour, lukewarm water, sugar, and salt.   Beat smooth with rotary beater.   Let stand, uncovered, at room temperature for 3 to 5 days, stirring 2 or 3 times each day. Cover at night to prevent drying.

To keep starter alive: Add 1/2 cup lukewarm water, 1/2 cup sifted Family Kitchen or Rose flour, and 1 teaspoon sugar to leftover starter. Let stand until bubbly and well-fermented, at least 2 days. Cover; refrigerate until used again.   If starter is not used within 2 weeks, add about 1 teaspoon sugar to keep it alive.   Repeat every 14 days.   NEVER STORE THE STARTER IN METAL.

NEVER-FAIL SOURDOUGH BISCUITS

1½ cups Family Kitchen or Rose FLOUR
2 teaspoons BAKING POWDER
¼ teaspoon BAKING SODA
½ teaspoon SALT
¼ cup melted BUTTER
1 cup SOURDOUGH STARTER BATTER

Sift the dry ingredients together.   Blend in butter and starter.   Pat the dough out on a floured surface, adding a little more flour, if necessary.   Cut in rounds or squares and place on greased baking sheets. Cover and let rise 30 minutes or until light. Bake in 425 oven for 20 minutes or until browned and done. (Makes one dozen biscuits.)

Pinto Beans

It is best to use soft water for bean cookery. To soften hard water, boil water vigorously for a period of 20 to 30 minutes in a closely covered kettle. This prolonged boiling will cause some of the calcium and magnesium salts to settle out.

To keep pinto beans from foaming up too high during cooking, add one tablespoon of salt pork drippings or other fat to the cooking water for each cup of beans.

BASIC PINTO BEANS

2 cups dry Rose brand PINTO BEANS
6 cups WATER
4 slices BACON
1½ teaspoons SALT
1 tablespoon SUGAR

Cook beans until tender. Add sugar and salt. Chip the bacon and brown in skillet. Add bacon and drippings to beans. Simmer one hour and serve hot.

WESTERN BAKED BEANS

3 cups PINTO BEANS
1 clove GARLIC, minced
1 or 1½ teaspoons SALT
2 small ONIONS
½ cup BROWN SUGAR or sorghum MOLASSES
1 teaspoon CHILE POWDER
¾ cup canned strained TOMATO
3 or 4 slices BACON or
½ cup diced SALT PORK

Wash the beans and cover them with water. Soak them overnight. Remove the beans from water. Heat to the boiling point the water in which the beans were soaked. Add the beans, garlic, and salt, and simmer one hour. Drain the beans, saving the liquid. Place the beans and whole onions in a pot or casserole. Sprinkle the beans with sugar or molasses and chile powder. Cover them with the tomato and one cup of the reserved bean liquid. Arrange bacon or diced salt pork or onion slices on top. Cover. Bake in a 300 oven for 5 hours.

JIFFY PINTO BEAN SALAD

2 cups cooked, drained Rose brand PINTO BEANS
3 hard boiled EGGS, chopped
2 tablespoons minced ONION
4 tablespoons minced PICKLE
1 teaspoon PREPARED MUSTARD
¼ teaspoon PEPPER
¼ cup MAYONNAISE
SALT to taste

Blend all ingredients. Serves 8 to 10 persons.

HOT BEAN SALAD

2 strips BACON, chopped, or 3 tablespoons diced
  SALT PORK
1/3 cup chopped ONION   ¼ cup VINEGAR
3 cups cooked BEANS   ¼ cup WATER
½ teaspoon MUSTARD   SALT and PEPPER

Brown bacon or salt pork in a large frying pan. Add onions and cook until lightly browned. Add beans, mustard, vinegar, and water. Simmer, stirring gently from time to time until the beans have absorbed the liquid. Season to taste and serve hot.

PINTO BEANS & BEEF

4 cups cooked Rose brand PINTO BEANS
1 cup TOMATO JUICE   2 teaspoons CHILI POWDER
1 cup diced CELERY   ½ teaspoon SAVORY SALT
1 medium ONION   ½ teaspoon GARLIC SALT
½ pound GROUND BEEF   1 tablespoon SUGAR

Combine cooked beans, tomato juice, onion, celery, and start them cooking. Fry ground beef in butter. Add spices. When beef is done, add to bean mixture and simmer about 30 minutes. Serve hot.

PINTO BEAN NUT BREAD

½ cup SUGAR   2 cups sifted FLOUR
½ cup SHORTENING   2 teaspoons BAKING POWDER
1 cup cooked Rose brand   ½ teaspoon CINNAMON
  PINTO BEANS   ¼ teaspoon NUTMEG
½ teaspoon SALT   ¼ teaspoon CLOVES
1 EGG   ¼ cup chopped NUTS

Mix and add ingredients in order given. Put in well-greased loaf pan and bake 45 minutes at 350.

PEGGY GOLDWATER BEANS

2 pounds **PINTO BEANS**
2 teaspoons **SALT**
2 large **ONIONS**
4 cloves **GARLIC**
½ teaspoon **BLACK PEPPER**

½ teaspoon **CUMIN SEED**
1 (4 oz. can) **TACO SAUCE**
1 (4 oz. can) roasted **GREEN CHILES**
1 #2½ can **TOMATOES**

Soak pinto beans in cold water overnight. Drain, wash, and cover with about 2 inches of water. Add salt and boil over moderate heat about an hour. (Add water as needed. Add diced onion and diced garlic, black pepper, cumin seed, chopped green chile, taco sauce and tomatoes. Cook over moderate heat for an hour or until beans are tender. For spicier beans, add one or two teaspoons of red chile powder.

For chile can carne, add chopped beef (about two pounds) sauteed until brown with a chopped onion in any kind of cooking fat and added to the beans after the hour of cooking.

RANCHO BEANS

1 pound **PINTO** or **KIDNEY BEANS**
WATER to cover
6 to 8 **PORK CHOPS**
¼ pound diced **SALT PORK**
1 chopped **ONION**
1 clove minced **GARLIC**
1 tablespoon **CHILI POWDER**
1½ teaspoons **SALT**
¼ teaspoon **PEPPER**

Soak beans overnight in water to cover generously. Cover pot and bring beans to a boil. Reduce heat and simmer until beans are almost tender (about 2 hours). Brown pork chops in fry pan. Remove and set aside. Add salt pork to pan and fry until lightly browned. Add onion and garlic and cook until tender but not browned. Remove from heat and stir in chili powder, salt and pepper. Add to beans, mixing well. Arrange browned pork chops on top of beans, cover and simmer 45 minutes longer (or until beans and chops are done). If needed, add a little more water while cooking. (Beans should have a little liquid but should not be soupy.) Serves 6.

RED FLANNEL STEW

2 tablespoons cooking FAT
1 large ONION, chopped
2 cups cooked PINTO BEANS
1 can CORNED BEEF (12 ounces)
1 can TOMATOES or TOMATO SAUCE
½ pound CHEDDAR CHEESE
CHILE POWDER
CORN TORTILLAS

Brown the chopped onions in cooking fat. Add cooked beans (1 cup) and mash into a paste. Add remaining beans, meat, chile powder, and tomatoes. Heat. Add cubes of cheese. Heat to melt. Serve on fried tortillas or use stew in place of beans for a chile burro.

BAKED PINTO BEANS

1 pound PINTO BEANS
6 cups WATER
3 tablespoonfuls BROWN SUGAR or MOLASSES
1 can TOMATOES
½ pound lean BACON
1/8 teaspoon OREGANO (crushed)
½ cup chopped ONIONS

Cook beans in water. Fry onions, browning them lightly in fat. Place cooked pinto beans in casserole. Add onions, brown sugar or molasses, canned tomatoes, salt and pepper, oregano and meat seasoning. Bake, covered in 325 F oven for thirty minutes. To brown: finish baking without cover.

MEXICAN CASSEROLE

3 cups cooked Rose PINTO BEANS
1 cup cooked or canned TOMATOES
2 tablespoons chopped GREEN PEPPER
GARLIC SALT
¾ cup chopped ONION
½ teaspoon SALT
1 teaspoon CHILI POWDER
4 strips BACON

Combine all ingredients, except bacon. Turn into greased baking dish. Arrange bacon strips over top. Bake at 350 for an hour.

PINTO BEAN LOAF

4 cups cooked Rose PINTO BEANS
3 canned PIMENTOS or 2 GREEN PEPPERS
1 tablespoon ONION JUICE
1 cup BREAD CRUMBS
2 EGGS (beaten)
MILK (for moistening)
SALT and PEPPER

Put cooked beans and canned pimientos or green peppers through a food chopper. Add onion juice, bread crumbs, beaten eggs, salt and pepper, and just enough milk to moisten the mixture. Mold and place in a greased loaf pan. Put strips of bacon across the top and bake about 50 minutes in a moderate oven. Turn the loaf on a platter, garnish with bacon and parsley and serve with hot tomato sauce.

(For variation--try adding a cup of ground cheese.)

BEST PINTO BEAN SOUP

3 cups dry Rose brand PINTO BEANS
2 HAM HOCKS or 2 slices HAM
1 cup diced ONIONS
1 cup diced CELERY
1 can TOMATO SAUCE
1 can TOMATO SOUP
SALT, PEPPER, and VEGETABLE SALT to taste

Cook beans with ham hocks or ham (diced). When almost done, add diced onions, celery, tomato sauce and soup. Add water as needed to make a medium thick soup.

PINTO BEAN FUDGE

2/3 cup CANNED MILK (light cream may be used)
1 2/3 cups SUGAR
1½ cups diced MARSHMALLOWS
½ cup chopped NUTS
½ cup strained (cooked) Rose brand PINTO BEANS
1½ cups CHOCOLATE CHIPS
1 teaspoon VANILLA

Combine sugar and milk in kettle. Boil five minutes, stirring constantly. Add remaining ingredients and stir until marshmallows dissolve. Pour in buttered pan. Cool and cut in squares.

Chili

Chiles have a thin, tough skin which can be removed. Try the oven or broiler method, or the blistering method for speedy results.

Oven or Broiler

Place peppers in hot oven or broiler (400 to 450) for 6 to 8 minutes. Remove from heat and allow to stand in a wet towel to steam for 15 minutes. Remove skin, stem, seeds, and membrane.

Blistering

Blister the skin of the peppers thoroughly on a hot range or with a flame, turning frequently to prevent scorching. Wrap the peppers in a towel and allow to stand for 10 minutes to steam and for the skins to soften. Slash skin and insert knife at tapered end, pulling the skin off toward the stem. Remove seeds and stems.

CHILE made from DRY RED CHILES

24 dried RED CHILES	2 tablespoons FLOUR
2 tablespoons FAT	1 teaspoon SALT
2 cloves GARLIC	1/2 teaspoon OREGANO
2 ONIONS	1 cup TOMATO JUICE

Wash 24 dry red chiles. Remove stems and seeds. Cover with water and boil for 30 minutes. Strain or put through a food mill. Saute onions, garlic, and add flour to make a smooth paste. Combine with chili paste. Add tomato juice, salt and oregano. Simmer for half an hour.

QUICK CHILI CON CARNE

1 pound Rose brand PINTO BEANS

3 tablespoons BACON FAT	2 pounds GROUND BEEF
½ cup chopped ONION	1 quart TOMATOES
	1 teaspoon CHILI POWDER

Wash and cook beans until tender. Heat bacon fat in skillet. Add chopped onion and ground beef. Brown and cook slowly for several minutes. Combine in a large kettle with tomatoes. Add chili powder to taste. Heat to boiling and serve.

CHILI CON CARNE #1

12 RED CHILES
1/2 teaspoon SALT
1/4 teaspoon OREGANO

1 lb. ROUND STEAK
1/4 teaspoon CUMIN SEED
1 small GARLIC BUD

Soak chiles, remove outer skin, mash well, then strain. Cut meat into small pieces. Put in greased skillet and cover. Cook slowly til almost done. Then add chile juice, salt, cumin seed, oregano, and garlic. Serve on hot fried tortillas.

CHILI CON CARNE #2

2 tablespoons SHORTENING
1 medium size ONION, chopped fine
1 clove GARLIC, minced
1 pound GROUND BEEF
1 tablespoon CHILI POWDER
½ teaspoon SALT

¼ teaspoon CAYENNE PEPPER
1/8 teaspoon black PEPPER
1 No. 2 can of TOMATOES
1 large can RED BEANS
2 tablespoons CATSUP

Melt shortening in a saucepan; add onion, garlic. Brown. Drain from the fat and remove from the pan. Then brown the beef. Return onions and balance of ingredients. Cover and simmer slowly for about 30 minutes, stirring occasionally.

CHILI CON CARNE #3

1½ cups DRY PINTO or PINK BEANS
½ cup diced SALT PORK
½ cup chopped ONION
1 clove minced GARLIC
½ pound ground lean MEAT
2 to 4 teaspoons CHILE POWDER
3 cups canned TOMATOES
SALT and PEPPER to taste

Soak and cook the dry pinto or pink beans. In another pan, fry diced salt pork until it is crisp. Brown the chopped onion and minced garlic in the pork fat. Add the fround lean meat, stir, and cook slowly for five minutes. Add 2 to 4 teaspoons of the chili powder. Combine the meat, onion, salt pork, and tomatoes with the cooked beans.

Add salt and pepper to taste and simmer until the meat is tender and the flavors are well blended. Serve at once. (Serves 6 to 8)

CHILI CON CARNE CON FRIJOLES

2 cups (1 package) Rose PINTO or RED KIDNEY BEANS
WATER for soaking
1 quart fresh WATER
1 tablespoon SALT
3 or 4 slices BACON
1 pound GROUND BEEF

2 tablespoons BACON DRIPPINGS
2 cloves GARLIC, crushed
1½ cans TOMATO PUREE
1 can undiluted CONSOMME
4 teaspoons CHILI POWDER
½ teaspoon OREGANO
¼ teaspoon SAGE
¼ teaspoon CUMIN SEED

Wash and pick over beans. In a deep bowl, cover beans generously with water and soak overnight. Drain. Cover and simmer beans in a deep, heavy, 4-quart kettle with one quart fresh water and one tablespoon salt, for approximately 1 1/2 hours.

Saute three or four slices of bacon in a skillet. Drain on paper toweling. Brown ground beef in the bacon drippings. Add this along with garlic, tomato puree, consomme, chili powder, oregano, sage and cumin seed. Re-cover and continue simmering.

Then saute the chopped onion and diced green pepper in the butter. When the onion and pepper are tender, add to the beans. Continue to simmer, covered for 2 1/2 to 3 hours, or until beans are tender. Season to taste with salt and pepper if necessary. Stir occasionally during cooking, but don't break up the beans too much. Pour into a serving dish. Garnish generously with crumbled bacon.

Harvey H. West & Tommie Vanover's CHILI

2 cups BEEF, cubed or chopped
2 large RED CHILI PEPPERS, peeled and chopped
1 medium ONION, chopped
Small chunk suet or ¼ cup OIL
1 clove GARLIC
2 or 3 CHILI TEPINS

2 teaspoons whole CUMINO
SALT, PEPPER
BROTH or WATER to cover

Brown beef with suet or in oil, add salt and pepper. Add onion, chopped chilis and enough broth or water to cover. Tie garlic, cumino and chili tepins in cheesecloth bag. Add bag of spices to boiling beef and simmer until tender. Remove bag and slightly thicken beef with flour and water.

GRANDPA'S CHILI CON CARNE

2 pounds GROUND BEEF or
  1 pound cubed ROUND STEAK
GARLIC SALT
1 cup CELERY with leaves
3 No. 303 cans TOMATOES
2 6-ounce cans TOMATO
  PASTE
2 tablespoons SUGAR
1 pound Rose brand PINTO
  BEANS (cooked)
½ cup PARSLEY
1 tablespoon WORCESTERSHIRE

1 can ripe OLIVES (pitted and
  quartered)
2 - 4 tablespoons
  CHILI POWDER
CAYENNE PEPPER
TABASCO SAUCE
Dash of OREGANO
BAY LEAF
GREEN PEPPER (optional)
½ cup chopped ONION

Coat beef with salt, pepper and garlic. Saute beef and celery in margarine. Cover and simmer for 10 minutes. Stir occasionally. Add tomatoes and paste, sugar, salt, pepper, beans, olives, oregano, parsley and Worcestershire sauce. Simmer 5-10 minutes. Taste and add remaining seasonings. Refrigerate overnight to improve flavor.

CHILI MEAT

5 pounds CHUCK or SIRLOIN BUTT
6 tablespoons VEGETABLE OIL
1 teaspoon SALT
¼ teaspoon PEPPER
¼ cup FLOUR
1 tablespoon POWDERED OREGANO

½ cup CHILI POWDER
3 to 4 cups cold WATER

Cut in cubes and dredge with flour. Brown in oil over medium heat. Add chili powder and oregano mixed with cold water. Cook from 4 to 6 hours. (This meat may be used in green and red chili recipes)

COMPANY CHILI

2 cans (15 ounce) Rosarita CHILI CON CARNE
4 peeled, quarted, fresh TOMATOES
3 chopped green ONIONS

Combine the ingredients and simmer slowly for 20-30 minutes. Serve in soup bowls with some chopped fresh green onions for garnish. Delicious with crisp corn tortillas or with heated flour tortillas and butter.

CHILI POR J. I. GARDNER

5 pounds BEEF CHUCK, ELK or VENISON
2 pounds PORK SHOULDER
1 large ONION
6 medium CLOVES GARLIC
12 to 16 RED CHILIS (dried)
1 tablespoon OREGANO
1 teaspoon CUMIN
1 teaspoon black PEPPER
SALT to taste

Trim all fat, gristle and bone from meat and cut into half-inch cubes. Cut all usable fat into small cubes and render until fat is brown. Lift out rendered fat pieces and save the grease for frying cubed meat. Saute meat until it has just left the red stage. (Do not over-fry.)

Wash red chili pods and remove stems and seeds. Soak chilis in hot water for 20 to 30 minutes. Pour water from chilis into blender and add chilis a few at a time. Blend until a creamy consistency.

Peel onion and garlic. Cut into small pieces and put into blender with enough oil to start onions and garlic to blend. Blend until creamy. Place in fry pan and saute until lemon colored.

Put all ingredients in pot large enough to hold ingredients, plus 6 or 8 cups hot water. Simmer until meat is tender.

Skim off excess oil and thicken with a thickening of flour or corn starch to desired consistency.

(NOTE: To add more "bite" add a small amount of cayenne or other hot chili. Be very careful about the amount you add; you want a zippy taste, not a burn.) This recipe freezes well.

SOUTHWEST CHILI

1½ pounds GROUND BEEF
1 chopped ONION
1 chopped GREEN PEPPER
1 clove minced GARLIC
3 (15½-oz.) cans RED BEANS
2 (6-oz. cans) TOMATO PASTE
1 tablespoon CHILI POWDER
2 teaspoons SALT

Brown the beef, onion, green pepper and garlic in a large frying pan. Drain fat. Mix in rest of ingredients. Simmer uncovered for 30 minutes. (Serves 5).

ALTA LAMB'S HOME-MADE CHILI

2 cups PINTO BEANS	½ cup KETCHUP
1 quart WATER	½ cup WATER
1 pound GROUND CHUCK	1 tablespoon SALT
2 tablespoons SHORTENING	2 tablespoons SUGAR
½ cup chopped ONIONS	2 tablespoons CHILI POWDER

Soak pinto beans in water overnight. In morning, wash beans twice. Cover with water and bring to a full boil. Simmer for 1 1/2 hours.

In a skillet, brown the meat until it turns gray. (Meat should be soft and crumbly, not hard). Mix in chopped onions, and stir continuously with fork. Add ketchup, water, salt, sugar, and chili powder. Simmer for half an hour. Add to beans and simmer 30 minutes more.

BEEF CHILI COMBO

2 pounds GROUND BEEF
2 medium-sized ONIONS, chopped
1 can (29 ounces) TOMATOES
1 can (16 ounces) KIDNEY BEANS
2 to 3 teaspoons CHILI POWDER
2 teaspoons SALT
1/8 teaspoon CAYENNE PEPPER
MASHED POTATOES, if desired

Cook beef and onion in large frying pan, stirring occasionally until lightly browned. Pour off drippings. Add tomatoes, beans, chili powder, salt, and cayenne pepper. Cover and cook slowly 30 to 40 minutes, stirring occasionally. Serve in bowls or over hot mashed potatoes.

Freezing

Line as many bowls as will be needed with heavy duty aluminum foil. Divide the chili into bowls. Cover tightly and freeze within the aluminum wrapping in the bowl. Freeze solid. Then lift package out and cover completely in foil. Return to freezer.

To reheat: remove package from freezer, remove foil. Place block of chili in top of double boiler over simmering water. Reheat, stirring occasionally until chili is completely heated (about 45-50 minutes).

Arizona Products

Arizona is a land of milk and honey... and beef, and dates, and citrus... and an abundance of food products processed in modern manufacturing plants.

Cattle ranchers are proud of their healthy beef stock; citrus growers boast oranges, desert grapefruit and lemons that are unsurpassed; date growers point with pride to their heavily-laden date palms; beekeepers buzz by with jars of glowing honey.

Citrus, in particular, identifies the plentitude of Arizona. Sour orange trees abound, the fruit ideal for marmalade and pie. Groves of oranges and grapefruit grow luxuriously -- the scent of orange blossoms permeating the dry, desert air. The fruit is unbelievably versatile -- citrus as a centerpiece, oranges eaten out of hand, lemons sparking spareribs and chicken; freshly-squeezed grapefruit juice to perk the appetite.

The fertile river valleys of Arizona produce a harvest of quality fruits and vegetables -- luscious melons, crisp carrots, tempting tomatoes, salad greens for sunshine salads.

Date palms thrive in Arizona's desert air, transplants from the Near East and North Africa. Dates are tucked into cookies and breads, served as party snacks, blended into cakes.

Blessed with sparkling sunshine, the richest of soils, and a sophisticated irrigation system, Arizona is a land of plenty.

Beef Bounties

BEEF EARTH ROAST

A Beef Earth Roast is an economical, easy and unusual way to feed a large group of people. Prepare as much or as little beef as you need for your group. Count on one pound of uncooked beef to serve two people. Freeze leftovers for use later.

1. Dig a pit 3' deep and 3' wide. Length depends on how much meat you cook. (A 10-foot pit will hold about 300 pounds of beef.)

2. Burn green hickory or oak limbs in this pit for 12 hours or until you have from 12" to 14" of live coals. Take all charcoal or unburned wood out.

3. Pour about 1/2" to 3/4" dry sand on the coals.

4. Cut beef into 4-lb. chunks and not more than 3" to 4" in depth. Wrap each piece of beef securely in aluminum foil. Then wrap in cheesecloth to prevent dirt from getting in.

5. Place beef on sand so the pieces lay separately and do not touch.

6. Come up 14" from the beef and place metal bars across the pit, 18" apart. Cover with overlapping tin so that the dirt and rain won't get in.

7. Take the dirt that you dug out of the pit and put over the top. Round the dirt off on top and ditch around it. Cover with a tarpaulin in case of rain.

8. Leave beef to slowly cook for 24 hours. When you uncover the meat it will be so tender that it can easily be pulled from the bones. Place meat in a large flat container and pour hot barbecue sauce over it.

LAZY POT ROAST

1 BEEF ROAST
1 package DRY ONION SOUP MIX
1 can CREAM OF MUSHROOM SOUP
½ soup-can WATER

Place an Arizona beef roast in a roaster, Dutch oven or casserole. Sprinkle a package of dry onion soup mix over meat. Add soup mixture. Cover and bake at 325 until tender (about 45 minutes per pound). Serve with the gravy that has formed.

BASIC BEEF MIX

2 pounds GROUND BEEF   Pinch SAVORY
2 cups cooked RICE   Pinch BASIL
2 teaspoons SALT   Pinch MARJORAM
½ teaspoon PEPPER

Combine beef with rice, salt, pepper, and a pinch each of savory, basil and marjoram.

BASIC TOMATO SAUCE

1 tablespoon FAT
1 large ONION, chopped
6 large TOMATOES, peeled and diced
1 tablespoon SUGAR   ½ teaspoon PEPPER
1½ teaspoons SALT   ¼ teaspoon ROSEMARY

Saute the onion in fat until wilted. Peel and dice tomatoes and add to onion, along with sugar, salt, pepper and rosemary. Simmer until tomatoes are tender (about 20 minutes).

STUFFED PEPPERS

Wash 4 green peppers, slice in half lengthwise and remove seeds. Place on a rack over boiling water in a large saucepan and steam until just tender. (Steam about 10-15 minutes). Stuff peppers with half of Basic Beef Mix. Top with half of tomato sauce. Top with breadcrumbs or wheat germ and grated cheese. Bake until meat is done (about 20 minutes) at 350.

CABBAGE ROLLS ARIZONA

1 medium head CABBAGE
1 tablespoon CARAWAY SEED   2 tablespoons BROWN SUGAR
½ teaspoon LEMON PEEL, grated   ¼ cup LEMON JUICE
BASIC BEEF MIX   BASIC TOMATO SAUCE

Core a medium head of cabbage. Place in a pan of boiling water until outer leaves are limp and can be peeled off. Remove leaves and drain. Add the caraway seed and lemon peel to 1/2 of basic beef mix. Place one tablespoon beef mix on each cabbage leaf. Roll and tuck in ends. Place rolls in a shallow baking dish. Add brown sugar and lemon juice to basic tomato sauce. Spoon sauce over rolls. Cover and bake at 350 for 20-30 minutes.

FRENCH-FRIED BEEF STRIPS

1 pound BEEF LIVER, sliced ½ inch thick
1/3 cup FLOUR
1 teaspoon SALT
1/8 teaspoon PEPPER
2 pounds FAT for deep-fat frying

Cut liver into strips, about 1/4 inch wide and 3 inches long. Combine flour, salt and pepper. Dredge liver strips in seasoned flour. Fry in deep fat (350) until brown for about 2-3 minutes. Drain on absorbent paper. Serve hot or cold.

SUPER BEEF LOAF

½ pound beef LIVER
3 slices BACON
2 large peeled ONIONS,
    quartered
1 LEMON RIND
2¼ pounds lean GROUND
    BEEF

¼ cup BREAD CRUMBS
¼ cup cold WATER
2 teaspoons SALT
½ teaspoon PEPPER
3 tablespoons chopped
    PARSLEY
1 EGG, beaten

Grind together the liver, bacon, onions and lemon rind. Mix with lean ground beef, bread crumbs, water, salt, pepper and parsley. Fold in the beaten egg. Pat into greased loaf pan and bake at 550 for 10 minutes or until brown and crusted on top. Reduce heat to 375 and bake for 45 minutes. Remove from oven and allow to rest 10 minutes for easier slicing.

MARSETTI

1 pound GROUND BEEF, lean
2 tablespoons FAT
1 small ONION, sliced
8 ounces broad NOODLES
2 8-ounce cans TOMATO SAUCE

¾ teaspoon SALT
2 teaspoons SUGAR
3 ounce can MUSHROOMS
½ pound mild CHEESE, cubed

Fry fat and stir in ground beef and onion. Cook until redness leaves the meat. Cook noodles according to package directions. Drain. Combine tomato sauce with salt and sugar. Layer the meat, noodles, and tomato sauce, along with mushrooms and cubed cheese, in casserole. Bake at 350 for 45 minutes.

BEEF MINESTRONE

1 clove GARLIC
2 tablespoons OLIVE OIL
1 package frozen MIXED VEGETABLES, cooked
½ cup CELERY, sliced
1 zucchini SQUASH, sliced
1 cup CABBAGE, shredded
1 can kidney, pinto or garbanzo BEANS
1 can TOMATOES
Leftover BEEF and NOODLES
SALT, PEPPER and OREGANO

Saute garlic in olive oil. Mix with vegetables and cook until tender. Add beans, tomatoes and leftover beef and noodles. Add salt, papper, oregano to taste.

TOP OF STOVE POT ROAST

1 BEEF ROAST
FLOUR
½ cup WATER (or STOCK or VEGETABLE BROTH)
¼ cup WHITE VINEGAR
1½ teaspoon SALT
¼ teaspoon PEPPER
½ teaspoon DRY MUSTARD

Dredge an Arizona beef roast with flour on all sides. Heat a heavy pan or Dutch oven over moderate heat. Brown roast slowly, using no fat. When brown, place a rack under meat. Add water, stock or broth and white vinegar. Cover and simmer over very low flame until tender. Half an hour before serving, add salt, pepper and mustard. Blend into juices, adding more liquid if desired. (This recipe produces a very BEEFY flavored roast).

BEEF & MAC COMBO

1 pound lean GROUND BEEF
¾ cup chopped ONION
½ cup chopped CELERY
1½ teaspoons SALT
1 cup uncooked MACARONI
1 cup shredded Cheddar CHEESE
1 can (1 pound 12 ounce) STEWED TOMATOES

In a 3-quart saucepan, saute the beef, onion and celery until meat is browned. Add tomatoes and salt; bring to boil. Stir in macaroni. Cover and cook over low heat, stirring occasionally, for 10 minutes or until macaroni is tender. Stir in cheese until melted.

CHILI POT ROAST

4 to 5 pound beef blade POT ROAST
2 tablespoons FLOUR
1 teaspoon CHILI POWDER
1 tablespoon PAPRIKA
2 teaspoons SALT
3 tablespoons LARD or DRIPPINGS

2 medium sized ONIONS
16 whole CLOVES
1/3 cup WATER
1 CINNAMON STICK
2 tablespoons FLOUR
¼ cup WATER

Combine flour, chili powder, paprika and salt. Dredge pot-roast in seasoned flour. Brown roast in lard or drippings. Pour off drippings. Stud each onion with 8 whole cloves. Add water, onions and cinnamon stick to meat. Cover and cook slowly for 2 1/2 to 3 hours or until tender.

Remove meat to hot platter. Discard onions and cinnamon stick. Measure cooking liquid and add water to make two cups. Mix flour and water. Add to cooking liquid and cook, stirring constantly, until thickened.

STUFFED FLANK STEAK

1 FLANK STEAK
½ cup CELERY, chopped
½ cup ONION, chopped
BASIC BREAD DRESSING
Liquid (WATER or MILK or STOCK)
2 tablespoons BEEF FAT, hot

1 teaspoon SALT
¼ teaspoon PEPPER
½ of a BAY LEAF

For each flank steak, add 1/2 cup each of chopped celery and onion to any basic bread dressing. Add enough liquid -- water, milk, stock -- to moisten. Spread on UNSCORED side of a SCORED flank steak.

Roll meat around dressing and tie securely with clean string. Brown on all sides in hot beef fat or other shortening. Add liquid, salt, pepper, half a bay leaf. Cover tightly, simmer, or bake at 325 for 1 1/2 hours.

COWBOY APPETIZER

(For instructions on preparing Beef Jerky, see Index.)

Toast several strips of jerky, after it is thoroughly dried, in a 450 oven, until it is hot and breaks easily. Break into small pieces and serve.

JERKY GRAVY

4 cups beef JERKY PIECES
3 tablespoons FAT
3 tablespoons FLOUR
2 cups MILK

Pound jerky pieces into flakes and powder. Use a heavy wooden mallet or hammer. Put pounded meat in Dutch oven with the fat. Over low heat, blend flour into fat. Cook and stir until the flour has thickened. Continue to cook slowly and stir constantly while adding the milk. Cook over moderate heat, stirring constantly until thickened. This gravy will probably not need seasoning as jerky will have retained its salt and pepper.

Serve on hot Dutch oven biscuits, or on plain boiled potatoes with jackets. Jerky is good on rice, boiled macaroni or mashed potatoes.

ROAST BEEF ENCORE

1 pound BEEF ROAST or POT-ROAST, cooked,
    cut in ¾" to 1" cubes
2 tablespoons SPAGHETTI SAUCE MIX from envelope
1 can (15 ounces) tomato sauce
½ cup WATER
2 packages (9 ounces each) frozen ITALIAN GREEN
    BEANS, cooked and drained
4 ounces NOODLES, cooked
¼ cup Parmesan CHEESE

Combine spaghetti sauce mix, tomato sauce and water in pan. Cook over low heat 5 minutes. Add beef cubes and cooked beans. Cook over low heat, stirring occasionally for 12 to 15 minutes or until beef is heated through. Serve on cooked noodles. Sprinkle Parmesan cheese over the top.

ARIZONA TERIYAKI

1 or more BEEF FLANKS
1 cup SOY SAUCE
3 tablespoons SALAD OIL
1 clove GARLIC, sliced
¼ teaspoon GINGER

Marinate one or more beef flanks for 30 minutes to all day (in refrigerator), in listed ingredients. Broil in moderate, preheated broiler 3-5 minutes on each side, basting during cooking with marinade. Slice thinly, diagonally across grain, topping with juices in broiler pan.

EASY ARIZONA CHILI BEEF

2 pounds lean boneless BEEF (chuck, stew, round,
   rump or brisket)
1 10-ounce can RED CHILI SAUCE (enchilada or taco sauce)
1 10½-ounce can BEEF BOUILLON

Cut beef into 1/2 inch pieces, trimming off fat.
Simmer beef, chili sauce, and bouillon in covered
pan, 45-60 minutes, until tender. If desired, thicken
sauce with 1 or 2 tablespoons cornstarch mixed to
a paste with cold water. (Makes 8 servings)

Serving ideas: (1) Chili beef may be served with
beans or rice.

(2) Cover bottom of shallow baking dish with
sauce from chili beef. Wrap chili beef in flour tortillas and place rolled tortillas in sauce. Sprinkle
with grated cheddar cheese and chopped green onions.
Heat in moderate oven (350) for 10-15 minutes, until
piping hot and cheese melts.

POTTED BEEF AND VEGETABLES

BEEF ROAST
1 tablespoon SALT
¾ teaspoon PEPPER
2 cloves GARLIC, minced

4 ONIONS, sliced
4 CARROTS, scraped and quartered
2 TOMATOES, quartered
2 BAY LEAVES

Mash salt, pepper, and garlic to a paste. Rub into
all sides of an Arizona beef roast. Place in roaster.
Surround with onions, carrots, tomatoes and bay
leaves. Cover and roast at 325 until tender (about
3 1/2 hours). Add water if roast gets too dry. Uncover last half hour if a browner crust is desired.
Potatoes may be added during last 45 minutes.

GRILLED FLANK STEAKS

1 or more BEEF FLANKS
SALT, PEPPER, BUTTER

Place one or more beef flanks, unscored as purchased, in moderate preheated broiler. Broil from
4-6 minutes on each side. Do not overcook!

Carve across grain diagonally into thin slices.
Season with salt, pepper and pat of butter. Top with
any meat juices left in broiler.

CHEESE 'n PRETZEL BEER LOAF

    1 cup BEER
    1 EGG YOLK
    ½ teaspoon SALT
    2 teaspoon melted BUTTER
    2/3 cup CHEDDAR CHEESE, shredded
    1 box HOT ROLL MIX
    2 tablespoons crushed PRETZELS

Preheat oven to 375.

Heat beer to warm. Put in large bowl. Sprinkle yeast from mix into warm beer. Stir to dissolve. Add egg yolk, salt, butter, cheese and hot roll mix. Blend well. Cover. Let rise in a warm place until double in bulk. Knead for 5 minutes on floured board. Place in greased 9x5x3 inch loaf pan. Cover. Let rise in a warm place until doubled in size.

Bake 30 minutes at 375. Remove from oven and brush with one egg white. Sprinkle with two tablespoons crushed pretzels. Bake 5 more minutes. Turn out on wire rack to cool.

SUPER BEER CAKE

½ cup BUTTER
1½ cups SUGAR
3 EGG YOLKS

2½ cups sifted all-purpose FLOUR
¼ teaspoon SALT
1 cup BEER
1 teaspoon VANILLA
½ teaspoon BAKING POWDER
3 EGG WHITES
1/8 teaspoon CREAM OF TARTAR

Preheat oven to 375.

Cream soft butter and sugar until fluffy. Add egg yolks, one at a time, beating well after each. Blend in sifted dry ingredients alternately with beer, beginning and ending with dry ingredients. Add vanilla. Sprinkle in baking powder. Beat egg whites and cream of tartar until stiff. Fold gently but thoroughly into batter. Grease and flour two 9-inch layer pans. Pour batter into pans.

Bake at 375 for 25 minutes or until cake tests done.

BEER, STEAK & MUSHROOMS

3 strips BACON, diced
1 pound SIRLOIN, sliced
1 clove GARLIC, minced
¼ pound fresh MUSHROOMS
¼ cup BUTTER
¼ cup FLOUR

1 cup CONSOMME
½ cup BEER
½ teaspoon SALT
¼ teaspoon THYME, ground
1 tablespoon PARSLEY, minced
1 BAY LEAF

Saute bacon in heavy skillet until crisp. Remove bacon. Brown meat in bacon fat. Remove. Saute mushrooms in fat. Remove. Melt butter, add flour. Slowly add consomme and beer, stirring until thick. Add remaining ingredients. Simmer one hour. Add more beer if thinner sauce is desired. Serve over wide noodles or rice.

PORK CHOPS BOHEMIAN

3 tablespoons COOKING OIL
6 PORK CHOPS
SALT and PEPPER
1/3 cup ONION, chopped
1 stalk CELERY, chopped

2 tablespoons FLOUR
1½ cups WATER
1/8 teaspoon SAVOR SALT
1 BAY LEAF
2/3 cup BEER

Heat oil in heavy skillet. Brown pork chops. Remove from pan. Generously salt and pepper each chop. Saute onion and celery in remaining fat. Add flour, stirring until browned. Gradually add water, stirring until well blended. Add pork chops, monosodium glutamate, bay leaf. Simmer 20 minutes. Add beer and simmer 20 minutes. Serve hot.

BEER CHILI

1 tablespoon BUTTER
1 pound GROUND BEEF
¾ cup ONION, chopped
1 No. 303 can TOMATOES
1 6-ounce can TOMATO PASTE
1 teaspoon SALT

¼ teaspoon PEPPER
1½ teaspoon CHILI POWDER
½ teaspoon PAPRIKA
1 can BEER
1 No. 303 can KIDNEY BEANS

Melt butter in heavy fry pan or Dutch oven. Add meat and onion. Cook until lightly browned, stirring frequently. Add remaining ingredients except kidney beans. Stir and cover. Simmer one hour, stirring occasionally. Add kidney beans. Simmer 20 minutes. Stir frequently. (Serves six.)

HONEY BEER CAKE

½ cup BUTTER
2 cups SUGAR
4 EGGS
½ cup ORANGE JUICE
½ cup APPLE BUTTER
¾ cup HONEY
4 cups sifted all-purpose
   FLOUR
2 teaspoons BAKING
   POWDER
¼ teaspoon SALT
1 teaspoon BAKING SODA
1 teaspoon NUTMEG
1 teaspoon CLOVES
1 teaspoon CINNAMON
1 teaspoon ALLSPICE
1 cup BEER
1 cup seedless RAISINS
½ cup BLACK WALNUTS,
   chopped

Preheat oven to 325.

Cream butter and sugar until fluffy. Add eggs, one at a time, beating well after each addition. Add orange juice, apple butter and honey. Mix well. Add sifted dry ingredients alternately with beer, beginning and ending with dry ingredients. Add raisin and nuts which have been coated with flour. Pour batter in greased and floured tube pan.

Bake at 325 for one hour and 20 minutes. Sprinkle top and sides with confectioners sugar.

CHERRY CAKE

4 EGGS
2 cups SUGAR
2 teaspoons VANILLA
2 cups sifted all-purpose FLOUR
2 teaspoons BAKING POWDER
¼ teaspoon SALT
2 tablespoons BUTTER, melted
1 cup BEER
1 cup MARASCHINO CHERRIES

Preheat oven to 375.

Beat eggs until thick and lemon colored. Gradually beat in sugar. Add vanilla. Fold sifted flour, baking powder and salt into egg mixture. Heat beer. Add beer and melted butter at once to batter. Pour into greased cherry-lined tube or molded pan. Bake at 375 for 30 minutes.

Turn out on cake rack to cool. Prick top of cake and drizzle with 4 tablespoons of warm beer.

Potato Chips

SCALLOPS & CHIPS SCOTTSDALE

2 lbs. SCALLOPS, fresh or
  frozen
1 cup light CREAM
¼ cup BEEF BROTH
  BOUILLON
2 teaspoons LEMON JUICE
½ teaspoon ONION, minced
¼ cup GREEN PEPPER, chopped

1 tablespoon chopped PIMENTO
½ teaspoon chopped PARSLEY
1 cup crushed POTATO CHIPS
SALT and PEPPER to taste
BUTTER
¼ cup chopped PINON NUTS

Mix cream, beef bouillon, lemon juice, onion, pepper, pimiento, parsley, salt and pepper and pour over scallops which have been arranged in a baking dish. Let these marinate (covered) in the refrigerator two to five hours for best flavor. Just before baking, add the crushed potato chips, pinon nuts and dot with butter. Bake 15 minutes in 450 oven.

CHIP STUFFING for SPARERIBS

1 ONION chopped fine
3 tablespoons SHORTENING
3 cups cubed BREAD
1½ cups crushed POTATO
  CHIPS

1 cup MILK or BOUILLON
4 pounds SPARERIBS
1 cup finely chopped APPLE
1 teaspoon SALT
½ cup chopped CELERY

Saute onion in shortening until tender. Combine with bread, potato chips, apple, celery, seasoning and milk. Cut spareribs in two matching sections; sprinkle with salt and pepper. Spread stuffing on one section, top with other section and tie with string, or fasten with skewers. Bake at 350 for about two hours.

CHIPPER LOAF

2 pounds GROUND BEEF
1 EGG slightly beaten
¼ cup minced ONION
¼ teaspoon PEPPER
1 can condensed VEGETABLE SOUP
2 cups crushed POTATO CHIPS

Combine all ingredients in a bowl and blend. Shape into a loaf and bake in shallow pan, uncovered, in a 350 oven for 1 1/2 hours.

Figs contain a small amount of acid; therefore, the fruit ferments easily. Two courses of preservation are open. One must either add large amounts of sugar to act as a preservative, combining this with long periods of cooking, or one must sterilize the product after canning.

In the preservation of fig products, it is recommended that the fruit be "blanched" from 5 to 10 minutes in boiling water. "Blanching" is pre-cooking in steam or boiling water.

DRIED FIGS

Steam or dip figs in boiling water for one or two minutes. (Peel if desired.)

Spread fruit (one-fig deep only) on wire screen or wooden slat trays covered with thin cheesecloth or other open fabric. Place in area with good air circulation, rather than in hot sun. Dry until the leathery stage (skin will be glossy, slightly sticky.) To hasten drying and keep insects away, use an electric fan. Store in glass jars or polyethylene bags in a cool spot.

FROZEN FIGS

Select soft, ripe fruit. Make sure they have not become sour in the center. Sort, wash and cut off stems. (Peel if desired). Cut in half or leave whole. Use 1/2 teaspoon ascorbic acid per quart of syrup to prevent discoloration. Freeze without sugar or cover with a cold syrup made from 2 1/2 cups sugar to 4 cups of water.

RHUBARB & FIG PRESERVES

3½ quarts RHUBARB
1 pint chopped FIGS
8 cups SUGAR
1 LEMON

Cut rhubarb into small pieces, add sugar and let mixture stand overnight. In the morning, boil until thick and add 1 pint of chopped figs plus the juice and rind of 1 lemon. Cook rapidly until mixture is thick and clear. Pack while hot into sterile, hot jars. Seal immediately.

QUICK FIG JAM

Figs for jam may be cut into small pieces or mashed. They may be peeled or unpeeled. If unpeeled, the pieces should be rather finely cut in order that a tender jam may result.

4 cups FIGS (mashed, cut, or sectioned)
4 cups SUGAR
6 tablespoons LEMON JUICE

Combine the sugar and the fruit. Add lemon juice. Place over a slow fire. When the mixture comes to a full boil, cook for 20 minutes. Remove from the stove and let set overnight in the pan in which it was cooked. The next morning, fill hot glasses with the cold jam.

(It is recommended that in all cases where cold mixtures are put into jars or glasses, paraffin should be poured on immediately, since the heat of the fat prevents molds and fermentation.

PICKLED FIGS (Short Method)

7 lbs. FIGS	1 teaspoon CLOVES
4 lbs. SUGAR	1 teaspoon ALLSPICE
1 pint VINEGAR	1 teaspoon CINNAMON
1 pint WATER	½ teaspoon MACE

(2 tablespoons whole spices may be used
instead of powdered spices, if preferred)

Blanch figs 5 to 10 minutes. Heat sugar and water and add vinegar and spices (either ground or whole). Boil 5 minutes. Remove spice bag. Add figs and cook until the fruit can be pierced with a toothpick and until penetration of syrup is complete. (This may take a half hour at a slow boil.) Fill sterilized jars and seal at once.

LEMON-FIG JAM

4 lbs. FRESH FIGS, peeled
3 lbs. granulated SUGAR
1 large LEMON, sliced thin

Mash or quarter the cleaned, peeled figs. Slice lemon very thin. Add sugar and lemon peel slices to figs and mix. Cook slowly stirring frequently with wooden spoon. Mixture will become thick and fruit transparent. Cooking process takes about 1 1/2 hours. Pour into sterile jars and seal immediately.

PICKLED FIGS (Long Method)

Blanch figs 5-10 minutes in boiling water. Make a syrup of the following:

1 cup **WATER**
1 cup **VINEGAR**
6 cups **SUGAR**
2 tablespoons mixed **PICKLING SPICES**
(tied in cheesecloth bag)

Use from 5 to 7 pounds of figs for this recipe. Boil the figs in syrup for 10 minutes for 3 consecutive mornings. Refrigerate the boiled figs daily. On the third day, pack into hot sterilized jars. Put on caps tightly and store.

Some canners prefer to place the hot capped jars in a water bath for 15 minutes to complete the sterilization.

(A boiling water bath is a process in which water is poured into a container deep enough to cover the top of jars one inch. A rack on the bottom of the container is needed to prevent jars from cracking. Bring the water to a boil and maintain this temperature for 110 minutes -- unless lemon juice is added. If lemon is added, process for 90 minutes. At the end of sterilization period, remove jars. Do not tighten tops if Kerr seals are used; tighten other types of lids.)

CANDIED FIGS

Select firm, undamaged figs for this process. They may be candied with skins on or peeled.

UNPEELED METHOD--Make a heavy syrup of two cups sugar and 1 cup water. Drop the cleaned fruit into this mixture and cook until tender to a straw or fork. Let stand 24 to 36 hours. Drain. Remove to drying racks. Turn fruit often and drain off extra syrup. When fruit is "gummy" but not "sticky" on the inside, and will not ooze syrup when squeezed, it is ready to be stored.

PEELED METHOD: Peel the fruit and proceed exactly as is indicated for unpeeled. For the best peeled product, use Mission or dark figs. The quality of peeled candied figs is improved if the pieces are rolled in granulated sugar just before serving. Do not roll in sugar during storage, as this tends to make the fruit sticky.

PYRACANTHA JELLY

1 full pint ripe PYRACANTHA BERRIES
2 pints WATER
Juice of 1 small GRAPEFRUIT
Juice of 1 small LEMON
1 package POWDERED PECTIN
5½ cups SUGAR

If a stronger flavor is desired, use 2/3 quart of berries. Boil berries and water, covered, for 20 minutes. Add juice of grapefruit and lemon. Strain juice to 4½ cups. Add pectin and bring mixture to boil. Add sugar and boil until it jells (about 4 to 5 minutes). Pour into sterile glasses and seal.

POMEGRANATE JELLY

4 cups POMEGRANATE JUICE
1 bottle LIQUID PECTIN
7½ cups SUGAR

Separate and crush edible portions of 10 to 12 fully ripe fruits. Do not remove seeds. Cook by adding a small amount of water. Place fruit in jelly bag and squeeze out juice. Measure sugar and juice into a large pan and mix. Bring to a rolling boil (one that cannot be stirred down). Add pectin, stirring constantly. Again, bring to full rolling boil and boil for one-half minute. Remove from fire, skim and pour into sterile glasses. Seal with paraffin at once.

APRICOT PIE

5 cups APRICOTS, halved
¾ cup SUGAR
¼ teaspoon NUTMEG
¼ teaspoon SALT

1 tablespoon FLOUR
1 tablespoon LEMON JUICE
1 tablespoon BUTTER

Topping
1 tablespoon BUTTER
3 tablespoon FLOUR
1 tablespoon SUGAR
¼ teaspoon SALT

Combine sugar, nutmeg, salt and flour. Sprinkle lemon juice over apricots. Arrange apricots and dry mixture in alternate layers in an UNBAKED pie shell. Dot with butter. Cover with top crust of unbaked pastry. Crumble topping ingredients and sprinkle over top. Bake at 425 for 10 minutes; reduce heat to 350 degrees and bake for 25 minutes.

Arizona Vegetables

CAESAR SALAD

3 quarts SALAD GREENS,
  bite-sized
½ cup SALAD OIL
½ cup Parmesan CHEESE
¼ cup BLUE CHEESE
1 tablespoon
  WORCESTERSHIRE SAUCE
½ teaspoon DRY MUSTARD
¼ teaspoon SALT
1/8 teaspoon PEPPER
1 EGG
½ cup fresh LEMON JUICE
2 cups crisp garlic-flavored
  CROUTONS

Put crisp, cold salad greens into large, chilled salad bowl that has been rubbed with a clove of garlic. Add oil, cheeses, Worcestershire, mustard, salt and pepper. Break raw egg over greens and pour in lemon juice. Toss very thoroughly so every leaf is coated with seasonings. On the last toss, add croutons. (Makes 8 servings.)

YUMA TOMATO SALAD

6 large ripe TOMATOES, quartered
½ cup PARSLEY, minced
½ cup GREEN ONION, minced
2/3 cup SALAD OIL
¼ cup RED WINE VINEGAR
¼ teaspoon SALT
1/8 teaspoon PEPPER
1 - 2 teaspoons DRIED BASIL
6 OLIVES (optional)
ICEBERG LETTUCE

In a deep crockery bowl, layer quartered tomatoes, parsley, and onion an hour before serving time. Blend together oil, vinegar, salt, pepper and basil. Pour over tomatoes, tilting bowl so all the tomatoes are covered. Refrigerate.

Drain off dressing into separate bowl. Arrange tomatoes on cold, lettuce-lined platter. Garnish salad with sliced olives, if desired. (Serves 6)

SUPER EGGPLANT

Remove stem; if skin seems tough, peel (otherwise panfry with skin). Cut into 1/2" to 1" slices or strips. Dip in flour, or fine dry bread or cracker crumbs. Then dip into an egg beaten with 2 tablespoons milk. Dip back into flour or crumbs. Fry in hot fat (olive oil is especially good) until brown on one side. Turn slices and brown on other side. Sprinkle with salt and Parmesan cheese and serve piping hot.

CARROT AMBROSIA

4 cups coarsely grated CARROTS
¼ cup fresh LEMON JUICE
1 can (3½ ounces) flaked COCONUT
2 to 3 tablespoons HONEY
¼ teaspoon SALT
½ cup SOUR CREAM
LETTUCE leaves

Put grated carrots into mixing bowl. Sprinkle with lemon or lime juice, then add coconut. (Save a small amount of coconut for garnish.) Toss.

Blend honey and salt with sour cream and add to carrot mixture. Toss. Line chilled salad bowl with lettuce leaves and add carrot salad. Garnish with coconut. (Makes 6 servings)

MELON MELBA

1 package frozen RASPBERRIES
¼ cup CURRANT JELLY
2 teaspoons CORNSTARCH
2 tablespoons WATER
1/8 teaspoon ALMOND FLAVORING
6 cups MELON BALLS or CHUNKS

Mix raspberries and jelly. Bring to a boil. Dissolve cornstarch in water. Add to raspberry mixture. Simmer several minutes until thick. Add almond flavoring. Cool.

Divide melon balls into 8 sherbet glasses. Spoon sauce over the top and serve.

WILTED LETTUCE

1 head LETTUCE
3 to 4 slices BACON, dried
½ cup WATER
½ cup VINEGAR
1 EGG, well-beaten
2 tablespoons SUGAR
½ teaspoon SALT
1 chopped GREEN ONION

Tear washed lettuce into bite-sized chunks into salad bowl. Fry bacon crisp in skillet. Leaving fried bacon in skillet, remove all but 1/4 cup of hot bacon fat. Add all other ingredients to bacon and fat. Bring to boil. Pour hot salad dressing over lettuce and toss lightly. (Also good on spinach leaves)

WESTERN VEGETABLE SALAD

½ cup OIL
¼ cup LEMON JUICE
2 teaspoons SUGAR
1 teaspoon SALT
½ teaspoon ground CUMIN
1 clove GARLIC, crushed

6 large TOMATOES
2 CUCUMBERS, peeled and
thinly sliced
2/3 cup ONION, minced
1 GREEN PEPPER, diced
1 cup (3 7/8 oz. can)
pitted ripe OLIVES

Prepare dressing by blending together oil, lemon juice, sugar, salt and cumin. Spear garlic on wood picks and put in dressing. Let dressing stand at least 2 hours before mixing with salad. Remove garlic. Makes 3/4 cup.

An hour before serving, cut tomatoes in 3/4" chunks. Mix with remaining salad ingredients in large salad bowl. Add enough dressing so vegetables are moist. Marinate for 1 hour. (Serves 8-10)

WESTERN STYLE SEAFOOD SALAD

1 cup SALAD OIL
1/3 cup tarragon VINEGAR
½ teaspoon SALT
1 clove GARLIC, minced
1 teaspoon DRY MUSTARD
1 teaspoon WORCESTERSHIRE SAUCE
1 head ICEBERG LETTUCE
½ head ROMAINE
½ pound cooked SHRIMP or CRAB LEGS
Freshly ground PEPPER

Prepare dressing by blending together oil, vinegar, salt, garlic, mustard and Worcestershire. Cover and chill in refrigerator. (Makes 1 1/2 cups dressing)

Prepare salad greens, cold and dry-crisp. Tear into bite-sized pieces. When ready to serve salad, add seafood and enough dressing to coat salad ingredients. Toss and garnish with pepper.

WESTERN SOUR CREAM DRESSING

1 cup SOUR CREAM
2 tablespoons VINEGAR
1 tablespoon fresh LEMON JUICE

1 tablespoon GREEN ONION
½ teaspoon SALT
3 tablespoons SUGAR

Blend together all ingredients and chill. Makes 1 1/4 cups of dressing.

Dairy Delights

LEMON-BANANA SHAKE

1 can (6 ounces) frozen LEMONADE concentrate,
    thawed
1 cup diced fresh BANANAS
3 cups MILK
1 quart VANILLA ICE CREAM

In a bowl combine lemonade concentrate and bananas; beat until jelly-like in consistency. For each milk shake, mix 1/4 cup milk, 1 scoop vanilla ice cream and 1/4 cup lemon-banana mixture in the bottom of glass. Fill glass 2/3 full with milk; stir until blended. Add 2 scoops ice cream.

ORANGE NOG

2 cups chilled MILK
1 cup chilled fresh ORANGE JUICE
3 tablespoons SUGAR
ORANGE slices (optional)

In a blender, mixer or with rotary beater, mix together milk, orange juice and sugar until foamy. Serve immediately. If desired, garnish each serving with an orange slice.

BANANA SPLIT FLOAT

2 ripe medium-sized BANANAS
3 cups cold MILK
1 package (10 ounces) frozen, sliced, sweetened
    STRAWBERRIES, thawed
1½ pints CHOCOLATE ICE CREAM

In a mixer or blender mash bananas. Add milk, strawberries and 1/2 pint chocolate ice cream; beat until just blended. Pour into tall chilled glasses and top each with a scoop of chocolate ice cream.

(For a variation, use 1 1/4 cups sliced, sweetened fresh strawberries for the frozen ones.)

STRAWBERRY MILK SHAKE

1 EGG   2 cups cold MILK
1 package (10 ounces) frozen STRAWBERRIES, thawed

In a blender or mixer combine milk, egg and strawberries.

PINEAPPLE-CHOCOLATE FLOAT

3 cups cold MILK
¼ cup CHOCOLATE SYRUP
1 can (6 ounces) PINEAPPLE JUICE concentrate, thawed
1 pint VANILLA ICE CREAM

Combine milk, chocolate syrup and pineapple juice concentrate; beat thoroughly. Pour into tall glasses and top each with a scoop of vanilla ice cream.

STRAWBERRY-PINEAPPLE COOLER

2 cups MILK
2½ cups (1 pound 4½ ounces can) chilled crushed PINEAPPLE
½ pint VANILLA ICE CREAM
1 pint STRAWBERRY ICE CREAM
MINT (optional)

In a mixer or blender combine milk, crushed pineapple and vanilla ice cream until just blended. Pour into tall glasses and top with a scoop of strawberry ice cream. Garnish with mint, if desired.

FROSTED MOCHA MILK

2 pints COFFEE ICE CREAM
½ cup CHOCOLATE SYRUP
¼ cup INSTANT COFFEE POWDER
2 quarts MILK

In a blender or mixer, beat ice cream, chocolate syrup, coffee and part of the milk until well blended. Combine with remaining milk and chill before serving.

MOCHA FROST

3 tablespoons COCOA
3 tablespoons SUGAR
2/3 cup WATER
1 tablespoon instant COFFEE POWDER
3 cups MILK
1 pint VANILLA ICE CREAM
WHIPPED CREAM (Optional)

In a saucepan, mix cocoa and sugar. Stir in water and cook about three minutes. Stir in coffee. Chill. Add milk and ice cream and beat in mixer or blender until well mixed and frothy. Pour into tall glasses and garnish with whipped cream, if desired.

COTTAGE MEAT LOAF

1 EGG, slightly beaten
1½ teespoons WORCESTERSSHIRE SAUCE
1 teaspoon SALT
¾ teaspoon DRY MUSTARD
1/8 teaspoon PEPPER
1¼ pounds GROUND CHUCK
1 cup COTTAGE CHEESE
½ cup minced ONION
¼ cup minced GREEN PEPPER

In a large bowl combine egg, Worcestershire sauce, salt, mustard and pepper. Add meat, cottage cheese, onion and green pepper. Mix lightly but thoroughly. Shape into a loaf in baking pan. Bake at 350 for 50-60 minutes. Let stand a few minutes before removing from pan to serve.

SKILLET MACARONI & CHEESE

¼ cup (½ stick) BUTTER
1 cup chopped ONION
1 tablespoon FLOUR
1½ teaspoon SALT
¼ teaspoon leaf OREGANO
1 package (7 or 8 ounces) elbow MACARONI
3½ cups MILK
2 cups (8 ounces) shredded Cheddar CHEESE

In skillet melt butter. Add onion and saute until tender. Stir in flour, salt and oregano. Add macaroni and milk. Cover and bring to boil. Reduce heat and simmer 15 minutes or until macaroni is tender, stirring occasionally. Add cheese and stir until cheese is melted. (Do not boil!)

BLUE CHEESE DRESSING

1 cup COTTAGE CHEESE
½ cup crumbled BLUE CHEESE
½ cup MILK
1 tablespoon LEMON JUICE
¼ teaspoon SALT

In a mixing bowl or blender, beat together cottage and Blue cheeses until fairly smooth. Blend in milk, lemon juice and salt. Cover and chill.

SWISS FONDUE

4 cups (1 pound) shredded aged Swiss CHEESE
¼ cup all-purpose FLOUR
1 clove GARLIC, halved
2 cups SAUTERNE
½ teaspoon SALT
½ teaspoon WORCESTERSHIRE SAUCE
Dash of ground NUTMEG

Toss together cheese and flour. Rub inside of saucepan with garlic. Discard garlic. Add sauterne and heat until bubbles rise. Over low heat add the cheese, 1/2 cup at a time, stirring until cheese is melted after each addition. Add salt, Worcestershire sauce and nutmeg. Transfer to fondue pot and serve with cubes of French bread.

CHEESE POTATO CASSEROLE

6 cups sliced cooked POTATOES
2 cups (8 ounces) shredded Cheddar CHEESE
2 EGGS, beaten   2 teaspoons SALT
1½ cups MILK   1/8 teaspoon NUTMEG

In casserole, layer half the potatoes and half the cheese. Repeat layers. In a bowl combine eggs, milk, salt, and nutmeg. Pour egg mixture over potatoes and cheese. Bake 30 minutes.

BREAD PUDDING

½ cup SUGAR
½ teaspoon CINNAMON
¼ teaspoon SALT
2 EGGS
1 quart (4 cups) fluid MILK
1 teaspoon VANILLA
8 slices BREAD, cut in cubes
½ cup seedless RAISINS
2 tablespoons BUTTER, melted

Mix sugar, cinnamon and salt in a large bowl. Beat in eggs and slowly stir in milk and vanilla. Stir in bread cubes, raisins and butter. Pour into 9-inch square pan. Bake at 350 about an hour, or until knife stuck near center comes out clean.

PECAN PIE

½ cup HONEY
½ cup BROWN SUGAR
¼ cup BUTTER

3 EGGS, beaten
1 cup PECANS
1 9" unbaked PIE SHELL

Blend honey and sugar together. Cook slowly to form a smooth syrup. Add butter. Add beaten eggs and pecans. Pour into pie shell. Bake in 400 oven for 8-10 minutes. Reduce oven heat to 350 and bake for 30 minutes, or until knife comes out clean.

HONEY BREAD PUDDING

2½ cups BREAD CUBES
2½ cups MILK
4 tablespoons BUTTER
½ cup HONEY
¼ teaspoon SALT
2 EGGS, slightly beaten
1 teaspoon VANILLA extract
¼ cup RAISINS

Scald milk and cover bread mixture. Let set for five minutes. Add butter, honey, and salt. Let cool several minutes. Pour mixture gradually over slightly beaten eggs. Add vanilla. Mix well and add raisins. Pour into greased baking dish. Place in a pan of hot water and bake in a moderate oven (350) for 50-60 minutes, or until firm.

CHERRY HONEY PIE

2 cups pitted CHERRIES
¾ cup HONEY
3 tablespoons TAPIOCA
1 tablespoon BUTTER
½ teaspoon CINNAMON
9" unbaked PIE SHELL and strips

Combine cherries, honey, and tapioca. Pour into pie shell. Dot with butter. Sprinkle with cinnamon. Cover with lattice-top crust. Bake in 450 oven for 10 minutes. Reduce heat. Bake in moderate oven (350) for 30 minutes.

HONEY-LEMON LAMB SPARERIBS

 ¼ cup BUTTER, melted
 ¼ cup HONEY
 ¼ cup LEMON JUICE
 1 teaspoon ROSEMARY, slightly crushed
 1 teaspoon ONION
 ½ teaspoon DRY MUSTARD
 ¼ teaspoon GARLIC POWDER
 3 to 3½ pounds LAMB SPARERIBS
 FLOUR, SALT, PEPPER

Combine butter, honey, lemon juice, rosemary, onion, garlic and mustard. Heat through. Sprinkle spareribs with flour, salt and pepper; rub in. Grill spareribs 5 to 6 inches from coals (5 minutes on each side). Then start basting spareribs with honey-lemon sauce. Baste and turn frequently for 20 to 25 more minutes.

LAZY DAY HAM

 1 thick-cut ready-to-eat HAM slice
 2 teaspoons DRY MUSTARD
 1/3 cup HONEY
 1/3 cup PORT WINE (or more as needed)

Rub ham slice with dry mustard, using 1 teaspoon mustard for each side. Place in a shallow baking pan. Combine honey and wine; pour over ham. Bake uncovered in a moderate oven (350) from 35 to 40 minutes.

HONEYED LAMB CHOPS

 4 loin LAMB CHOPS (1-inch thick)
 ¼ cup HONEY
 2 teaspoons SOY SAUCE
 ¼ cup LEMON JUICE
 4 ONION slices

Combine soy sauce, honey, and lemon juice. Mix well. Add lamb and chill one hour, turning occasionally. Remove lamb. Reserve honey mixture. Broil lamb 3 to 4 inches from source of heat for six to seven minutes. Turn and top with onion slices and broil six to seven minutes longer. Brush lamb with honey mixture frequently during cooking.

HONEY MUFFINS

2 cups all-purpose FLOUR
1 teaspoon SALT
3 teaspoons BAKING POWDER
1 cup MILK
4 tablespoons HONEY
1 EGG, beaten
¼ cup melted SHORTENING

Sift flour with salt and baking powder. Combine milk, honey, egg, and melted shortening. Add to sifted flour mixture. Stir quickly, long enough to merely moisten dry ingredients. Fill greased muffin tins one-half full. Bake at 400 for 25-30 minutes or until browned. (Makes dozen muffins)

ORANGE-HONEY MUFFINS

2 cups sifted all-purpose FLOUR
1 tablespoon BAKING
  POWDER
¾ teaspoon SALT
2 tablespoons freshly grated
  ORANGE PEEL
¼ cup HONEY
1 EGG, well beaten
¾ cup MILK
¼ cup freshly squeezed
  ORANGE JUICE
¼ cup melted SHORTENING
2 ORANGES, peeled and
  sectioned (16 sections)
2 tablespoons SUGAR

Sift together flour, baking powder and salt; add grated peel. Combine honey, egg, milk, orange juice and melted shortening. Add to sifted dry ingredients all at once. Stir quickly and vigorously until the dry ingredients are just mixed and have a lumpy appearance. Fill greased muffin pans 2/3 full. Place an orange section on top of each muffin and sprinkle with sugar. Bake at 425 for 25 minutes. (Makes 16 muffins).

ORANGE HONEY BUTTER

½ cup (1 stick) BUTTER
2 tablespoons HONEY
2 tablespoons frozen concentrated ORANGE JUICE

In small mixing bowl, cream butter until softened. Gradually add honey and beat until light and fluffy. Continue beating while slowly adding orange juice concentrate. Serve on pancakes, waffles, French toast or toasted English muffins. (Makes 3/4 cup)

ORANGE MARMALADE

4 medium sized (or 3 large) unpeeled
ORANGES (halved and sliced thin)
4 unpeeled LEMONS (sliced thin)
Granulated SUGAR

Measure oranges and lemons together. Add 5 times as much cold water. During next 24 hours, boil hard for an hour. This will reduce the quantity one-half. Measure into 4-cup units. (Cooking in this quantity will produce better flavor). If oranges are overly sweet, add 1 tablespoon lemon juice for every cup of fruit. Bring to boiling point. Boil 8 minutes. Add 3/4 cup sugar for each cup of fruit.

Boil first unit rapidly until it jells -- not more than 10 minutes. If a longer time seems to be necessary, boil the next unit for a longer time before the sugar is added. Pour into sterilized glasses and cover with paraffin when cold.

TANGY ORANGE MARMALADE

3 thin-skinned ORANGES
2 LEMONS (or LIMES)
1½ cups WATER
1/8 teaspoon BAKING SODA
6 cups SUGAR
½ of 6-oz. bottle LIQUID PECTIN

Wash fruit; remove peel in quarters, and cut into fine slivers. Add water and baking soda. Bring to a boil. Cover and simmer 20 minutes, stirring occasionally. Dice pulp, discarding center membrane and seeds. Add pulp and juice to undrained rind. Cover. Simmer for 10 minutes. Measure 3 1/2 cups of the mixture into a large saucepan. Add sugar and mix well. Place over high heat; bring to a full rolling boil and boil hard 1 minute, stirring constantly. Remove from heat; stir in pectin immediately. Skim off foam with a metal spoon; alternate stirring and skimming for 7 minutes. Ladle into hot sterilized jars and seal with paraffin.

3-DAY MARMALADE

5 SOUR ORANGES
1 GRAPEFRUIT
Granulated SUGAR

1st day

Cut sour oranges and grapefruit in half and remove the seeds. Cut the pulp and rind in slices. Measure. Add 3 times as much water as fruit. Let the mixture stand.

2nd day

Boil the mixture for 20 minutes at a hard boil. Set mixture aside for the next day.

3rd day

Measure the mixture and measure an equal amount of sugar. Boil the fruit for 20 minutes, and add sugar all at once. Stir. Boil 35 minutes (or until a little jells on a cold saucer). Seal with paraffin while hot.

SOUR ORANGE MARMALADE

2 pounds SOUR ORANGES
(about 6 medium sized)
2 quarts WATER
3 pounds SUGAR
½ teaspoon SALT

Remove the peel from two oranges. Slice this peel very thin and cover with water. Boil until tender, adding additional water as it boils away. (Change the water often if the flavor becomes too bitter).

Peel the remaining oranges (the peel may be stored in freezer for later grating uses). Boil the pulp in 2 quarts water until very soft. Strain through a bag with pressure. Re-strain without pressure. Mix this juice with the drained peel, the sugar and the salt and boil until the jelly stage is reached. Let stand until slightly cool. Stir and pour into hot sterilized jars and seal with paraffin.

●

At your next holiday party, make a pinata -- a thin earthenware jar covered with papier mache to form a fanciful animal or clown, and decorated with colorful tissue paper. Fill the pinata with oranges, nuts, candy, and toys.

SOUR ORANGE MARMALADE

1 lb. SOUR ORANGES, peeled
1/3 of PEEL (removed from oranges)
2 pints WATER
1½ lbs. SUGAR

PREPARATION OF PEEL: Wash fruit, remove peel, discard two thirds of the peel, reserving the best third. With a knife, remove any blemishes that may appear. Cut this peel into thin slices. Place in a kettle and add water (four times weight of peel). Boil for ten minutes, then drain. Repeat this process from three to five times, each time boiling the water for five minutes. Peel should be tender. (Bitter taste may be removed by changing the water a sufficient number of times.)

PREPARATION OF THE JUICE: After the peel has been removed, weigh the remaining fruit, cut into small pieces, place in a kettle, and for each pound of orange taken add 2 pints of water. Boil until it thoroughly disintegrates. Pour into a flannel jelly bag and press until no more juice can be obtained. Strain this juice again through a clean flannel jelly bag without pressing.

MAKING THE MARMALADE: Pour this juice into a kettle, add peel, and bring to a boil. Add 1 1/2 pounds of sugar for each pound of fruit. Continue the boiling until the jellying point has been reached (indicated by flaking or sheeting from spoon). Cool and pour into sterile jars; seal with paraffin.

LEMON SAUCE

3 tablespoons CORNSTARCH
½ cup SUGAR
¼ teaspoon SALT
2 cups WATER

1 tablespoon grated LEMON PEEL
3 tablespoons LEMON JUICE
¼ cup BUTTER or MARGARINE

Mix together cornstarch, sugar, and salt in a small saucepan. Gradually stir in water and cook and stir over low heat until mixture comes to a boil, thickens and becomes clear. Remove from heat and stir in lemon peel and juice and butter. Cool slightly. Serve over shortcake or pudding. (Makes 2 1/4 cups).

CITRUS MARMALADE

2 large or 3 medium GRAPEFRUIT
4 large or 6 medium ORANGES
2 large LEMONS
4 cups COLD WATER
10 cups SUGAR (approx.)
3 pieces GINGER ROOT
1 tablespoon pure VANILLA EXTRACT

Wash grapefruit, oranges and lemons. Cut in thin slices, remove seeds and cut each slice into 1/4-inch strips. Measure fruit. There should be about 7 cups grapefruit and 5 3/4 cups oranges.

Place fruit in deep kettle. Add water to cover. Bring to a boiling point. Drain. Repeat twice. Add 4 cups cold water, bring to a boil, reduce heat and simmer, uncovered, 1 1/2 hours or until fruit is tender.

Measure fruit. Add sugar (1 cup for each cup fruit.) Add ginger root. Cook over low heat, stirring frequently, about 2 1/2 hours or until thickened. Add pure Vanilla extract. Remove from heat and fill sterilized jars.

CLEAR ORANGE MARMALADE

6 ORANGES
3 LEMONS
Granulated SUGAR

Slice oranges and lemons very thin. Cover the fruit with water in heavy saucepan and allow to stand overnight. Next day, boil 40 minutes and again set overnight. Measure fruit the next day. For every cup of fruit, add 1 1/2 cups sugar. (About 7 cups of fruit is used in this recipe). Bring to a boil and simmer 40 minutes. Pour into sterile glasses while hot. Seal with thin layer of paraffin; add more paraffin later.

ORANGE - CRANBERRY RELISH

2 ORANGES, unpeeled   1½ cups BROWN SUGAR
1 lb. fresh CRANBERRIES   ½ cup chopped WALNUTS

Trim thin slice from both ends of oranges. Cut in half lengthwise. With a shallow "V" shaped cut, remove white center core. Cut into chunks and whirl in covered electric blender until smooth. Add cranberries, blending until smooth (or put through food grinder). Stir in sugar and nuts. Chill.

POT-OF-GOLD MARMALADE

1 large seedless ORANGE
6 cups canned sliced PEACHES (two 1-pound-13 ounce cans)
3½ cups SUGAR
½ teaspoon each of SALT and GROUND GINGER
    (if preferred, NUTMEG or other spice may be used)
2 tablespoons LEMON JUICE

Chop or cut orange into tiny pieces. Then cook with 1 1/2 cups water until peel is soft. Add more water if needed to finish cooking. Drain peaches and cut into about 1/2 inch pieces before measuring.

Combine all ingredients, including water in which orange is cooked. Boil rapidly, stirring often, until there is very little free liquid and the mixture will round slightly on a spoon. (The mixture thickens after cooling.)

Pour boiling-hot marmalade to within about 1/8 inch of top of jelly jar. Wipe off anything spilled on top or threads of jar. Put dome lid on jar. Screw band or cap tight.

CITRUS BEEF POT ROAST

1 (4-to-5 lb.) boneless RUMP ROAST
2 tablespoons DRIPPINGS or OIL
2 teaspoons SALT
¼ teaspoon PEPPER
¼ cup WATER
1 tablespoon BROWN SUGAR
1 teaspoon COCOA
¼ teaspoon MACE
¼ teaspoon CINNAMON
6 tablespoons frozen ORANGE JUICE concentrate, thawed
2 thin LEMON SLICES
2 medium ORANGES, sliced but not peeled
¼ cup WATER
¼ cup FLOUR

Brown meat in drippings. Pour off drippings. Season meat with salt and pepper. Add water, cover tightly and cook slowly two hours.

Combine sugar, cocoa, mace, cinnamon and two tablespoons orange juice concentrate and add to meat. Add lemon slices. Cover tightly and continue cooking from 1 to 1 1/2 hours. Add orange slices and continue cooking 5-10 minutes, or until heated through.

Remove meat and orange slices to warm platter. Remove lemon slices and discard. Blend remaining 4 tablespoons orange juice concentrate, water and flour and use to thicken cooking liquid for gravy.

CANDIED CITRUS PEEL

3 cups CITRUS PEEL, cut into strips from:
4 to 5 medium Sunkist ORANGES, or
6 medium Sunkist LEMONS, or
2 medium to large Sunkist GRAPEFRUIT
12 cups cold WATER
2½ cups SUGAR
½ cup HONEY
1¾ cups boiling WATER

Wash fruit. Score peel into quarters. Remove sections of peel with fingers; cut into uniform strips about 3/8 inches wide. Boil peel with 6 cups cold water, uncovered, for 10 minutes. Drain and rinse. Repeat process with 6 cups fresh water.

In a large saucepan, combine 1 1/2 cups sugar, honey and boiling water. Bring to a boil and boil about one minute. Add cooked, drained peel and briskly simmer until almost all of the syrup has been absorbed, about 30 to 40 minutes. Stir frequently to avoid sticking.

Transfer peel to collander. Drain well, about 10 minutes. In large bowl, toss drained peel with remaining 1 cup sugar to coat well. Spread pieces out on waxed paper to dry. Store in tightly covered container.

CITRUS TEA COOLER

3 TEA BAGS or 1 tablespoon loose BLACK TEA
1½ cup boiling WATER
½ cup fresh LEMON JUICE
1 bottle (28 ounces) LEMON-LIME CARBONATED
    BEVERAGE or GINGERALE, chilled
¾ to 1 cup SUGAR
1 tray ICE CUBES
½ cup fresh ORANGE JUICE

Place tea bags or loose tea in bowl. Pour boiling water over tea. Let stand 5 minutes. Remove bags or strain to remove leaves. Add sugar and stir until all is dissolved. Place ice cubes in 2-quart serving pitcher. Pour hot tea, lemon and orange juice over tea. Stir briskly several seconds until mixture is cold. Stir in chilled lemon-lime carbonated beverage. Pour into glasses and serve at once. (Makes 2 quarts)

SOUR ORANGE MERINGUE PIE

7 tablespoons CORNSTARCH
1¼ cups SUGAR
6 tablespoons SUGAR
¼ teaspoon SALT
2 cups WATER
1 tablespoon BUTTER

3 EGG WHITES
3 EGG YOLKS, slightly beaten
1 tablespoon sour orange RIND, grated
1/3 cup sour orange JUICE
1 baked 9-inch PIE SHELL

Mix cornstarch, 1 1/4 cups sugar and salt in a one-quart saucepan. Stir in water slowly and mix until smooth. Cook on low until mixture is thick, stirring constantly; continue cooking until mixture is very thick and smooth. Stir small amount of cornstarch mixture into egg yolks, return to saucepan and cook constantly. Remove from fire. Add butter, rind and juice; blend. Cool to room temperature. Pour filling into pie. Beat egg whites until stiff. Beat in sugar gradually. Continue beating until stiff. Pile lightly on pie filling in shell to make complete seal. Be sure it's spread to an even thickness over the whole pie. Bake in 325 F oven for 25 minutes. Cool before serving.

SOUR ORANGE PRESERVES

4 SOUR ORANGES
1½ cups sour orange JUICE
1½ cups WATER
1½ cups SUGAR

Wash sour oranges. Peel off thin yellow skin, leaving as much of thick white part as possible; cut in halves. Squeeze out juice. Handle carefully to avoid splitting halves. Cover with water in a large saucepan and cook 10 minutes. Drain. Make a syrup of orange juice, water and sugar. Drop halves into syrup. Cook on low heat until rinds are transparent. Pack rinds in clean jars. Cover with hot syrup. Seal and place jars in large kettle of hot water. The water should cover jars. Simmer for 10 minutes to complete the seal and sterilize.

●

Do you know what the navel on an orange means? It's your clue to an orange with no seeds, an orange that peels easier than other oranges, an orange that breaks easily into bite-sized sections.

FRESH GRAPEFRUIT CAKE

(2 layer cake)

2 cups sifted CAKE FLOUR
1¼ cups SUGAR
2 teaspoons BAKING POWDER
½ teaspoon SALT
5 EGGS, separated
¼ cup fresh squeezed GRAPEFRUIT JUICE
1/3 cup WATER
1/3 cup SALAD OIL
1 tablespoon fresh grated GRAPEFRUIT PEEL
¼ teaspoon CREAM OF TARTAR

Sift together dry ingredients. In small mixer bowl, combine egg yolks, grapefruit juice, water and oil. Add dry ingredients. Beat at low speed until blended. Then beat at medium speed for one minute. STIR in grapefruit peel. Beat whites until frothy; add cream of tartar. Continue beating until whites are stiff, BUT NOT DRY. Carefully fold yolk mixture into whites until just blended. Pour into 9-inch layer cake pans lined with oiled waxed paper. Bake at 350 for 25-30 minutes. Leave in pans 10 minutes. Turn out onto wire rack to cool. Frost.

ORANGE-APRICOT BREAD

½ cup DRIED APRICOTS
1 ORANGE
½ cup RAISINS
½ cup chopped NUTS
2 teaspoons BUTTER
1 1/3 cups SUGAR

1 teaspoon VANILLA
1 EGG
2 cups sifted FLOUR
2 teaspoons BAKING POWDER
¼ teaspoon SODA
¼ teaspoon SALT

Soak apricots in enough cold water to cover for 1/2 hour. Squeeze juice from orange into a measuring cup and add enough boiling water to make a cup. Put orange skins, drained apricots and raisins through a food chopper. Cream butter and sugar, add vanilla, egg, and fruit mixture and beat smooth. Add dry ingredients alternately with orange juice and water, blending after each addition. Bake at 350 degrees an hour in a greased and floured pan (9 x 5).

NESSELRODE PIE

½ cup SUGAR
2 envelopes unflavored GELATINE
½ teaspoon SALT
3/4 cup freshly squeezed ORANGE JUICE
¼ cup WATER
3 EGGS, separated.
1 tablespoon freshly grated ORANGE PEEL
3 medium California ORANGES, peeled
¼ cup chopped DATES
¼ cup finely chopped CANDIED CITRON
½ cup heavy CREAM, whipped
Toasted COCONUT CRUST
ORANGE PEEL Poinsettia

In saucepan, thoroughly combine 1/4 cup sugar, gelatine and salt; stir in orange juice and water. Beat egg yolks slightly; blend into mixture until smooth. Cook over medium heat for five minutes, stirring until gelatine is thoroughly dissolved. Stir in orange peel. Chill until mixture mounds very slightly when dropped from a spoon. Meanwhile, cut peeled oranges into small pieces and drain well. Fold oranges, dates and citron into gelatine mixture. Beat egg whites to soft peak stage; gradually add remaining 1/4 cup sugar and continue to beat at high speed until stiff, but not dry. Carefully fold whites and whipped cream into filling; spoon into Toasted Coconut Crust. Chill until set. Garnish with Orange Peel Poinsettia.

Toasted Coconut Crust

1 tablespoon BUTTER or MARGARINE
1¼ cups flaked COCONUT

Soften butter. Spread evenly over bottom and sides of 9-inch pie plate. Press coconut evenly into butter to form shell. Bake at 325 for 10-15 minutes, or until golden. Chill thoroughly.

Orange Peel Poinsettia

Pour hot water over orange; let stand 5 minutes. Score peel into quarters. Remove with fingers. With kitchen shears or paring knife, cut into poinsettia shape. Let stand in water until ready to use.

ZESTY ORANGE BREAD

¾ cup slivered ORANGE RIND (4 oranges)
1½ cups SUGAR
1/3 cup WATER
3 tablespoons BUTTER or MARGARINE
1 1/3 cups ORANGE JUICE
3 EGGS, well-beaten
4 cups sifted all-purpose FLOUR
4 teaspoons BAKING POWDER
½ teaspoon BAKING SODA
2 teaspoons SALT

Wash and dry oranges. Remove thin orange rind with a sharp knife. Cut rind into very thin slivers with scissors or knife. Combine sugar and water. Add rind and stir constantly over low heat until sugar is dissolved. Cook slowly for five minutes. Peel and syrup should measure 1 1/3 cups.

Add butter. Stir until melted. Add orange juice and beaten eggs. Sift flour, baking powder, soda, and salt together into mixing bowl. Add orange mixture and stir to moisten. Batter will be lumpy.

Grease and line with wax paper a 9x5x3 loaf pan. Pour batter into prepared pan. Bake at 325 degrees one hour and 15 minutes. Turn out on rack to cool. (Makes one loaf).

ORANGE MOLASSES BREAD

¾ cup SUGAR
4 cups sifted all-purpose
 FLOUR
1 teaspoon SODA
3 teaspoons BAKING
 POWDER
2 teaspoons SALT
1 1/3 cups coarsely chopped
 NUTS

1 cup EVAPORATED MILK
2 tablespoons grated
 ORANGE RIND
¾ cup ORANGE JUICE
3 tablespoons melted
 SHORTENING
¾ cup unsulphured MOLASSES

Sift together sugar, flour, soda, baking powder, and salt. Add nuts. Combine evaporated milk, orange rind, orange juice, shortening, and molasses. Add to flour mixture all at once. Stir just to blend. Turn into a greased and wax-paper lined 9x5x3 loaf pan. Bake at 325 degrees for one hour and 15 minutes. (Makes one loaf.)

SPICY ORANGE NUTS

1½ cups unsifted powdered
   SUGAR
2 tablespoons CORNSTARCH
1 teaspoon CINNAMON
¾ teaspoon CLOVES
¼ teaspoon ALLSPICE
1/8 teaspoon SALT

2 tablespoons freshly grated
   ORANGE PEEL
2 EGG WHITES, slightly
   beaten
3 tablespoons freshly squeezed
   ORANGE JUICE
2 cups WALNUT or PECAN
   halves

Sift together sugar, cornstarch, spices and salt. Stir in grated peel. Blend egg whites with orange juice; stir in nuts, coating each half completely. Drain thoroughly. Then roll in sugar mixture to coat well. Spread on cookie sheet. Do not allow nuts to touch. Bake at 250 for 20 to 25 minutes (or until dry). Cool before storing in covered container.

ORANGE PEANUT BUTTER CAKE

2 2/3 cups SIFTED FLOUR
1 cup GRANULATED SUGAR
2 teaspoons BAKING SODA
¾ teaspoon CINNAMON
¼ teaspoon SALT
2/3 cup BROWN SUGAR,
   packed

1 cup PEANUT BUTTER
2 EGGS (large)
1 1/3 cup fresh ORANGE
   JUICE
1 ORANGE
1/3 cup BROWN SUGAR,
   packed

Sift together flour, granulated sugar, baking soda, cinnamon, and salt into large bowl. Add 2/3 cup brown sugar, peanut butter, eggs and orange juice. Stir gently to mix, then beat about 100 times until batter is smooth. (Or, beat at medium speed with electric mixer until batter is smooth).

Grate 1 tablespoon of peel from orange. Peel orange, cut into fine pieces and drain. Stir orange pieces and peel into batter. Pour batter into greased and floured 13 x 9 x 2 inch cake pan. Sprinkle 1/3 cup brown sugar evenly over top of batter.

Bake at 325 for 45 to 50 minutes, until cake tests done. Cake is done if it springs back when touched lightly in center. Serve warm or cool.

EASY ARIZONA FRUITCAKE

4 cups RAISINS
2 cups ORANGE JUICE
1 cup BUTTER
2 cups ORANGE
  MARMALADE
1 teaspoon grated LEMON
  RIND
1 tablespoon grated ORANGE
  RIND
1 teaspoon BAKING SODA
½ cup ORANGE JUICE

4 cups sifted Family Kitchen
  or Rose FLOUR
1 teaspoon NUTMEG
1 teaspoon ALLSPICE
2 teaspoons CINNAMON
½ teaspoon SALT
3 EGGS
2 cups pitted, chopped DATES
2 cups chopped WALNUTS
1 pound candied FRUIT MIX

Grease a 10-inch tube pan, line it with waxed paper and grease the paper. In a large saucepan combine raisins, 2 cups orange juice, and butter. Place over direct heat and bring to a boil, stirring occasionally. Reduce heat and simmer for 10 minutes. Remove from heat and cool.

When mixture is cooled, stir in marmalade and grated rind. Dissolve baking soda in the 1/2 cup orange juice and add to mixture. If the saucepan is large enough, you may mix everything in the pan. If not, turn mixture into a large bowl. Sift together flour, spices, and salt; stir into the mixture along with the remaining ingredients. Mix well with a large wooden spoon or clean hands. Turn batter into prepared pan and bake in 300 oven 3 to 3 1/2 hours, or until cake tests done. Cool in the pan.

When cake is thoroughly cooled, remove pan and then carefully remove the paper. Wrap the cake in cheesecloth and then seal in plastic wrap or a plastic storage bag. Age cake at least four weeks in a cool, dry place before serving.

●

FRESH CITRUS GARNISHES

From unpeeled citrus cartwheel slices, you can prepare:

Curls

Cut half of fruit from cartwheel, leaving entire peel. Curl peel to center.

Cartwheel Twists

Cut cartwheel just to center; twist.

Fluted Cartwheels

Cut notches around the peel with sharp paring knife or kitchen shears.

STRAWBERRY-ORANGE JAM

2 ORANGES
4 cups STRAWBERRIES
(about 3 boxes)
7 cups SUGAR
½ bottle liquid PECTIN

Cut unpeeled oranges into very thin wedges. Remove ends and seed as necessary. Put in saucepan, cover with water and boil 15 minutes. Drain and repeat with fresh water. Drain thoroughly and chop or dice. Combine oranges and crushed berries in a large saucepan. Add sugar and mix well. Place over high heat; bring to a full rolling boil and boil hard one minute, stirring constantly. Remove from heat and stir in pectin immediately. Stir and skim for 5 minutes to cool slightly and prevent floating fruit. Ladle into hot sterilized jars and seal immediately with hot paraffin.

ORANGE-BANANA NUT BREAD

2½ cups sifted all-purpose FLOUR
4 teaspoons BAKING POWDER
¾ teaspoon SALT
¾ cup Chopped NUTS
1½ cups mixed CANDIED FRUITS
1/3 cup RAISINS
½ cup SHORTENING
¾ cup SUGAR
3 EGGS
½ cup mashed BANANA
½ cup ORANGE JUICE

Sift together flour, baking powder, and salt. Stir in chopped nuts, candied fruits, and raisins. Cream shortening, add sugar, beat until light and fluffy. Add eggs, one at a time, beating after each addition. Combine mashed banana and orange juice; add to creamed mixture alternately with flour mixture, beginning and ending with dry ingredients. Turn into a greased, wax-paper-lined 9x5x3 loaf pan. Bake at 350 degrees 1 1/4 hours. Cool 20 to 30 minutes before turning out on cake rack. (Makes one loaf.)

LEMON BAKED CHICKEN

1 frying CHICKEN (3 lbs.)
GARLIC SALT
1 teaspoon OREGANO, crushed
1 teaspoon grated LEMON PEEL
¼ cup fresh LEMON JUICE
¼ cup WATER

Cut chicken into serving pieces. Sprinkle chicken pieces with garlic salt. Place in shallow baking pan, skin-side-down. Combine oregano, lemon peel and juice and water and pour over chicken. Bake, uncovered, at 400 for 15 minutes. Turn chicken.
Continue to bake. Baste with pan drippings once or twice. Bake for about 40 minutes or until fork tender. Pan drippings may be used over chicken or rice. (Makes 4 to 6 servings)
(Note--garlic powder or a clove of garlic can be used with salt when garlic salt is not available.)

ICED LEMON SOUFFLE

3 envelopes unflavored GELATIN
1½ cups SUGAR
9 EGGS, separated
1 cup plus 2 tablespoons LEMON JUICE
¾ cup WATER
3 tablespoons grated LEMON PEEL
¾ teaspoon SALT
Additional LEMON PEEL and SUGAR

Mix gelatin and 3/4 cup sugar in top of double boiler. Add slightly beaten egg yolks, lemon juice and water to gelatin mixture. Cook and stir over simmering water until gelatin dissolves and mixture thickens slightly. Add lemon peel and remove from heat. Chill, stirring occasionally, until mixture begins to set.
Add salt to egg whites and beat to soft peaks. Gradually add remaining 3/4 cup sugar, beating until stiff glossy peaks form. Gently fold in gelatin mixture. Pour into lightly oiled 1-qt.-souffle dish with a 4-inch oiled collar.
Chill 3 to 4 hours. Carefully remove collar. Mix lemon peel with a small amount of sugar and pat mixture onto collar. Garnish top with a lemon slice.

GOLDEN WEST FRUIT CAKE

1 cup BUTTER or MARGARINE
2 cups SUGAR
4 EGGS
4 cups sifted FLOUR
1½ teaspoons SODA
1½ cups BUTTERMILK
1½ cups WALNUT or PECAN
  halves
1½ cups pitted snipped DATES
¾ cup sliced CANDIED
  CHERRIES

¾ cup diced CANDIED PINEAPPLE
¾ cup freshly grated ORANGE PEEL

1¼ cups SUGAR
2 tablespoons freshly squeezed
  LEMON JUICE
2 tablespoons freshly grated
  ORANGE PEEL
1 cup freshly squeezed
  ORANGE JUICE

Cream butter well. Gradually add sugar, beating until fluffy. Add eggs, one at a time, beating well after each addition. Beat in 1 cup flour. Stir soda into buttermilk. Add to creamed mixture alternately with remaining flour, beating until smooth. Stir in nuts, dates, candied fruit and 1/4 cup orange peel. Pour into well greased 10 inch tube pan. Bake at 325 for 2 hours, until cake tests done. To prevent overbrowning, place a piece of foil on top of cake during the last 45 minutes of baking. Cool on wire rack 10 minutes.

Meanwhile, combine remaining ingredients in a saucepan; briskly boil 1 minute. Remove cake from pan; pierce entire surface with fork. Slowly spoon hot syrup over cake until all the syrup is absorbed. Cool before slicing. Stores well in refrigerator if tightly wrapped with foil.

ORANGE SLAW

3 medium or 4 small ORANGES
1 small head CABBAGE (1¾ lbs.)
¼ small ONION

1 tablespoon SUGAR
½ teaspoon SALT

¾ cup MAYONNAISE
1 tablespoon fresh LEMON JUICE

Peel oranges and cut into bite-size pieces. Shred cabbage, using long blade on grater or cut finely with sharp knife. Chop onion finely. Place oranges, cabbage and onion in large serving bowl.

Mix together mayonnaise, lemon juice, sugar and salt. Pour over slaw and mix lightly. Cover and refrigerate 20 to 30 minutes before serving.

Date Delights

DATE CAKE

1 pound DATES, pitted
1 cup hot WATER
1 teaspoon SODA
1 cup SUGAR
2 tablespoons BUTTER

1½ cups sifted FLOUR
½ teaspoon BAKING
POWDER
1 teaspoon VANILLA
1 EGG, beaten
½ cup SOUR MILK
½ cup NUTMEATS

Cut dates fine. Sprinkle soda over dates and pour hot water over all. Let stand, while creaming sugar and butter. Add beaten egg, vanilla and milk alternately with dry ingredients. Add nuts, and mix date mixture into batter. Blend well and bake in 350 oven 35 to 40 minutes.

TOPPING

1 cup DATES
1 cup SUGAR
¾ cup WATER

1 tablespoon BUTTER
1 tablespoon CORNSTARCH
½ cup chopped NUTS

Cook all ingredients until thick (about 5 minutes). Remove from heat, and add nuts. Cool and spread on cake.

SOFT DATE CLUSTERS

2 cups fresh DATES
½ cup SHORTENING
1 cup SUGAR
1 EGG
1 teaspoon VANILLA

2 cups sifted FLOUR
1 teaspoon SALT
½ teaspoon BAKING SODA
½ cup BUTTERMILK

Cut dates into small pieces. Cream shortening with sugar. Beat in eggs and vanilla. Sift flour with salt and soda. Blend into creamed mixture alternately with buttermilk. Stir in dates. Drop by teaspoonfuls onto greased baking sheet. Bake in 375 oven 10-12 minutes, until lightly browned at edges. (Makes 5 dozen 2" cookies.)

•

To cut dates easily, wet a pair of kitchen scissors and snip away.

DREAMY BLIND DATES

40 DATES
40 WALNUT MEATS
¼ cup BUTTER or
  MARGARINE
½ teaspoon VANILLA
¾ cup BROWN SUGAR
1 EGG, beaten

1¼ cups Family Kitchen FLOUR
¼ teaspoon SALT
¼ teaspoon BAKING SODA
¼ teaspoon CREAM OF
  TARTAR
¼ teaspoon NUTMEG
¼ cup SOUR CREAM

Pit dates and fill each with a walnut meat. Refrigerate while you prepare cooky batter. Cream butter with vanilla gradually blending in sugar. Stir in egg. Sift together flour, soda, salt, cream of tartar and nutmeg. Add to creamed mixture alternately with sour cream. When blended drop three or four filled dates into batter; coat well. Lift on to greased baking sheet. Bake at 450 for 10 minutes. (Makes about 40 filled cookies.)

DATE BALLS

1 8-ounce package pitted DATES, chopped
½ cup seedless RAISINS
1 cup chopped WALNUTS
45 VANILLA WAFERS, rolled fine
¼ cup BROWN SUGAR
¼ cup BRANDY
2 tablespoons WHITE CORN SYRUP
Flaked COCONUT

Combine all ingredients except coconut. Roll into balls. Roll balls in coconut until well coated. (Makes about 45 balls)

FRESH LEMON-DATE PIE

1 cup fresh diced DATES
4 LEMONS
1 cup SUGAR

½ cup sifted all-purpose FLOUR
Unbaked PASTRY for double
¼ cup WATER

Pare the lemons, making sure to remove white membrane. Slice lemons. Combine sugar and flour. Line a 9-inch pie plate with half the pastry. Sprinkle a layer of sugar mixture on pastry shell. Then add a layer of lemon slices and a layer of diced dates. Repeat layers, ending with lemon slices. Sprinkle with water. Arrange remaining pastry over top. Bake in 400 oven about 40 minutes.

DATE-NUT BREAD

1½ cups cut-up DATES	1 teaspoon BAKING SODA
1½ cups boiling WATER	½ teaspoon SALT
2 tablespoons BUTTER	1 EGG
2¾ cups sifted FLOUR	1 cup chopped NUTS
1 cup SUGAR	

Pour water over dates. Then add the butter and let stand at room temperature. Sift dry ingredients. Add to date mixture and mix. Add egg. Mix well. Add chopped nuts. Bake in loaf pan at 325 degrees for one hour and 15 minutes.

BUTTERMILK SKY DATE CAKE

1¾ cups sifted Family Kitchen or Rose FLOUR	1½ cups SUGAR
1 teaspoon BAKING SODA	1 cup SALAD OIL
½ teaspoon SALT	3 EGGS
½ teaspoon NUTMEG	1 cup BUTTERMILK or SOUR MILK
1 teaspoon CINNAMON	2 teaspoons grated LEMON RIND
½ teaspoon CLOVES	

1 cup chopped WALNUTS
1 cup chopped, pitted DATES

Grease and flour a 9x13 inch pan. Sift flour with baking soda, salt, and spices. Set aside. Combine sugar, oil, and eggs. Beat until smooth. Add the sifted dry ingredients to the sugar mixture alternately with the buttermilk or sour milk. Stir in the lemon rind, nuts, and dates. Pour batter into prepared pan and bake in 300 oven for 55 to 60 minutes, or until cake tests done. Cool in the pan, on a rack. Spread with favorite icing.

DATE CANDY

2 EGGS
¼ cup BUTTER
1 cup SUGAR
1½ cup finely chopped DATES
2 cups BREAKFAST CEREAL, chopped NUTS
or COCONUT

Beat eggs with fork in cold fry pan. Add butter, sugar and dates. Simmer. Add breakfast cereal, crumbled. Stir well, turn out on waxed paper. Butter hands and make little balls. Roll in chopped nuts, coconut or more breakfast cereal.

ORANGE DATE CAKE

½ cup hydrogenated FAT
2 cups SUGAR
4 EGGS
3½ cups FLOUR
½ teaspoon SALT

1 teaspoon BAKING SODA
1¼ cups BUTTERMILK
2½ cups (1 lb.) pitted, cut DATES
1 tablespoon grated ORANGE RIND
1 cup NUTS, chopped

Cream together the shortening and sugar. Beat in eggs, one at a time. Sift the flour, salt and soda together and add them in alternately with the buttermilk. Mix the dates, orange rind and nuts together. Then, blend them into the mixture.

Pour batter into a lightly greased and floured 12-inch tube pan. Bake at 350 for an hour.

Topping

1 cup ORANGE JUICE
2 cups SUGAR
1 tablespoon grated ORANGE RIND (optional)

Mix ingredients, dissolving sugar, and bring to a boil. Set aside. As soon as the cake is taken from the oven, slowly pour this mixture over the top, punching holes in the cake with a long-tined fork or pick. Leave the cake in the pan at least five hours (or overnight) to absorb the juice. Store covered cake in refrigerator.

HONEY DATE BARS

½ cup SHORTENING
1 cup HONEY
1 teaspoon VANILLA
1¼ cups Family Kitchen FLOUR
3 EGGS
1 teaspoon BAKING POWDER
½ teaspoon SALT
1 cup DATES
1 cup NUTS
CONFECTIONER'S SUGAR

Blend shortening, honey and vanilla until creamy. Beat in eggs one at a time. Blend in sifted dry ingredients. Add nuts and dates--stir just enough to distribute evenly. Spread into a greased 9x9 inch pan. Bake at 350 for 30 to 35 minutes. Cool. Cut into one-inch length bars and roll in confectioners sugar. (Makes about 3 dozen 1x3 inch bars)

SOUTHWESTERN CAKE

1¾ cups sifted Family
   Kitchen or Rose FLOUR
1 teaspoon BAKING SODA
½ teaspoon SALT
½ cup BUTTER or
   MARGARINE
1 cup BROWN SUGAR
½ cup granulated SUGAR

2 EGGS, separated
1 teaspoon VANILLA
   EXTRACT
½ cup BUTTERMILK or
   SOUR MILK
1 cup mashed BANANAS
½ cup chopped, pitted DATES
½ cup chopped WALNUTS

Grease and flour a 9-inch square pan. Sift flour with baking soda and salt. Set aside. Cream butter until light and then gradually add the sugars, beating until mixture is light and fluffy. Beat in egg yolks and vanilla. Combine buttermilk or sour milk with mashed bananas. Add the sifted dry ingredients to the creamed mixture alternately with the banana mixture. Blend in dates and nuts. Beat egg whites until stiff and fold them in last. Turn batter into prepared pan and bake in 350 oven for 45 minutes, or until cake tests done. Cool on rack, in the pan. When completely cool, top with favorite frosting.

DATE PUDDING

½ cup SUGAR
1 EGG beaten
1 cup DATES
½ cup WALNUTS

¼ cup FLOUR
½ teaspoon SALT
½ teaspoon BAKING POWDER

Mix sugar and eggs thoroughly. Add remaining ingredients. Put into greased shallow baking dish. Bake at 350 for 30 minutes. Serve warm or cold with hard sauce or whip cream.

DATE-CHEESE DROP BISCUITS

1 cup DATES
2 cup BISCUIT MIX
½ cup soft AMERICAN CHEESE SPREAD or
   grated AMERICAN CHEESE
¾ cup MILK

Cut dates into medium-size pieces. Combine biscuit mix and cheese. Add milk and dates. Stir to moderately soft dough. Drop by spoonfuls onto greased baking sheet. Bake in 425 oven 10-15 minutes. Serve hot. (Makes about 18 biscuits)

STEAMED FIG or DATE PUDDING

1 cup FIGS or DATES, firmly packed	2 tablespoons MILK
1 cup BEEF SUET	1 teaspoon BAKING SODA
½ cup RAISINS	1 teaspoon SALT
2 cups dry BREAD CRUMBS	¾ teaspoon CINNAMON
2 EGGS, well-beaten	½ teaspoon NUTMEG

1 cup finely packed Spreckles Light Brown SUGAR

Chop figs or dates and suet fine. Mix with rest of ingredients and pack into medium-sized mold or pudding pan, greased well. Cover tightly with lid or several layers of foil. Set mold in a kettle and add enough boiling water to reach the two-thirds mark on the mold. Cover tightly and steam for two hours. Add more boiling water as it boils away. Serve warm with Hard Sauce.

HARD SAUCE

½ cup BUTTER
1½ cups Spreckles Powdered SUGAR
1 EGG YOLK
1 teaspoon VANILLA EXTRACT or 1 to 2 tablespoons RUM or COGNAC

Cream butter until very soft. Add sugar gradually and continue whipping until mixture is very smooth. Add egg yolk and flavoring and beat smooth. If you like a thinner sauce for spooning over cake or pudding, add a little boiling water. (Makes 1 1/2 cups)

DATE NO-COOK RELISH

1½ cup fresh DATES
¼ cup sweet pickle RELISH
¼ cup BROWN SUGAR
¼ cup CATSUP
1 teaspoon DRY MUSTARD
¼ teaspoon SALT
1 can PINEAPPLE tidbits

Cut dates into quarters. In a bowl combine all ingredients EXCEPT dates and pineapple. Mix well. Gently stir in dates and pineapple, including pineapple syrup. Cover and refrigerate several hours to blend flavors. Serve with poultry, pork or beef.

Prickly Pear

Beware of stickers when preparing this fruit. Wear heavy gloves and use metal tongs to handle the pears. Pick the fruit in October, or when it has attained the maximum redness for best flavor and color. Flavors of prickly pears will differ. The sugar, acid and pectin of the fruit varies with its ripeness. For best results, prepare only small quantities at one time.

To remove stickers, here are some suggestions:

1) brush pears with a vegetable brush.

2) put fruit in a pan and pour hot water over it. This dissolves a film and stickers fall off.

3) wash pears with a spray hose to remove the spines and rinse.

4) rub pears with heavy cloth or singe.

PRICKLY PEAR JELLY #1

> 10 pounds PRICKLY PEARS
> 12 cups SUGAR
> ¾ cup LEMON JUICE
> 2 bottles CERTO

Place fruit in a kettle and mash. Barely cover with water and simmer for two hours, adding water as necessary. Pour into a cloth bag through which the juice will drain. Add sugar and lemon juice. Stir and bring to a boil; let boil two minutes. Add two bottles of Certo. Skim off foam and pour jelly into sterile jars. Seal immediately.

PRICKLY PEAR PUREE

Force the raw fruit pulp through a food mill or a medium-fine wire strainer to remove seeds and heavy fibers. The puree may be packed into containers and frozen for future use. (Thaw before using in a recipe.)

PRICKLY PEAR SALAD DRESSING

> ½ cup PRICKLY PEAR PUREE
> 1/3 cup SALAD OIL (not olive oil)
> 1 teaspoon seasoned SALT
> 1 teaspoon SUGAR
> 3 to 4 tablespoons white wine VINEGAR

Shake all ingredients together in a covered jar or beat with a rotary beater. Makes about one cup of pink dressing. Serve on fruit or tossed green salads.

PRICKLY PEAR JELLY #2

2½ cups PRICKLY PEAR JUICE
1¾-ounce pkg. POWDERED PECTIN
3 tablespoons LEMON or LIME JUICE
3½ cups SUGAR.

Rinse the fruit and place in kettle, adding enough water to cover. Boil until quite tender (about an hour). Press with a potato masher to break skins. Strain through a jelly bag or two thicknesses of cloth.

To 2 1/2 cups of juice, add one 1 3/4-ounce package of POWDERED pectin (not liquid) and bring to a fast boil, stirring constantly. Add 3 tablespoons lemon or lime juice, and 3 1/2 cups sugar. Bring to a hard boil and cook for 3 minutes at a rolling boil.

Remove from fire. Add red food coloring (if desired) after skimming, and pour into sterile jelly glasses. Seal immediately with paraffin.

PRICKLY PEAR MARMALADE

4 cups chopped PRICKLY PEARS
1 cup sliced LEMON
2 ORANGES
SUGAR

Wash fruit and remove spines. Cut lemon into paper thin slices. Measure. Chop orange peel and pulp. Add 4 cups water to lemon and orange. Let stand 12 to 18 hours in a cool place. Boil until peel is tender. Cool. Pare, chop and measure pears. Measure lemon, orange and water in which cooked. Add 1 cup sugar for each cup pear, lemon, orange and water. Boil to jellying point. Pour, boiling hot, into hot jar; seal at once.

PRICKLY PEAR PRESERVES

2 quarts PRICKLY PEARS
1½ cups SUGAR
5/8 cup WATER
2½ tablespoons LEMON JUICE
1 slice of ORANGE (¼ inch thick)

Prepare two quarts of prickly pear cactus fruit by removing the skins, cutting in halves, and removing the seeds. Cook the cactus fruit until transparent in a syrup made of sugar, water, lemon juice and slice of orange. (Remove orange slice before packing preserves in jar.) Remove from heat and seal.

CACTUS CANDY #1

Select prickly pear cactus (or small barrel cactus if you own this type of cactus, since it's illegal to remove it from the desert). Remove spines and outside layer with large knife. Cut pulp across in slices one-inch thick. Soak overnight in cold water. Remove from water, cut in one-inch cubes and cook in boiling water til tender. Drain. Cook slowly in the following syrup until nearly all the syrup is absorbed. Do not scorch!

SYRUP for 2 QUARTS of CACTUS CUBES

3 cups granulated SUGAR
1 cup WATER
2 tablespoons ORANGE JUICE
1 tablespoon LEMON JUICE

Heat all ingredients until sugar is dissolved, then add cactus. Remove cactus from syrup, drain and roll in granulated or powdered sugar. For colored cactus candy, any vegetable coloring may be added to the syrup.

CACTUS CANDY #2

Cut cactus into one-inch slices. Take out the core and remove the rind, as only the pulp is used. Cube pulp and cover it with water. Boil for about 5 hours. Drain thoroughly. Make a solution that is 50 per cent sugar and 50 percent white corn syrup. This mixture should cover the pulp. Cook pulp and syrup for an hour. Allow it to stand until the next day.

On the third day, cook syrup until it threads. It should look like preserves when ready to crystallize. Take another kettle and make a fresh mixture, using 2 parts sugar to 1 part corn syrup. Stir and cook this fresh mixture until it is a little cloudy. While still cloudy, take cactus pulp and drop each piece into mixture for about 2 minutes. (Several pieces may be dropped in at one time.) Remove with tongs and place on a piece of screen where it will drain. Do not put the pieces of cactus too close together as they will form a solid mass.

Outdoor Arizona

Almost any day in Arizona is a good day for backpacking, camping, or relaxing in the patio. Rugged souls will slip a lightweight pack on their backs and head for the "trail." Camping enthusiasts will outfit a camper and meander along the highway until they spot an ideal campground. Patio picnickers will slip into comfortable clothes and enjoy their backyard barbecues.

For backpackers, the emphasis in foods is on compactness, nourishment, and durability. Dehydrated products are invaluable; they may be purchased at supermarkets and backpacking stores. However, many backpackers prefer to prepare high-energy foods at home in advance of their trek. To speed meal preparations, pre-measure, mix and pack in small plastic bags what will be required for individual meals.

Mixtures of fruits, nuts, seeds, and chocolate chips for munching are generally preferred in lieu of a noonday meal on the trail. They provide quick pick-me-ups and are easy to fix in advance.

The major difference between backpackers and campers is the emphasis on equipment. Campers generally come prepared to do extensive cooking outdoors. Camp cookery can range from the simple opening of cans to tasty meals prepared from scratch.

In preparing this section of the ARIZONA COOK BOOK, we were so impressed by the interest in recipes for the outdoors that we are now planning an entire book featuring all types of outdoor cooking -- recipes for cooking wild game and fish, for ranch parties, for pool parties, for pit barbecuing, etc. If you have a recipe you'd like to submit, please send it to our publishers. Your help will be very much appreciated.

Backpacking Bracers

ALMOND BARS

½ cup BUTTER or
   MARGARINE
½ cup BROWN SUGAR
½ cup quick-cooking OATS
½ cup whole wheat FLOUR
   (unsifted)
½ cup all purpose FLOUR
   (unsifted)

¼ cup WHEAT GERM
2 teaspoons grated ORANGE
   RIND
2 EGGS
1 cup whole blanched
   ALMONDS
¼ cup RAISINS
¼ cup flaked COCONUT
½ cup semi-sweet
   CHOCOLATE BITS

Cream butter with 1/2 cup brown sugar until soft; beat in oats, flours, wheat germ and orange rind. Pat into 8 inch square pan. Then mix eggs, almonds, raisins, coconut, chocolate bits and 1/4 cup brown sugar (packed). Pour over base and spread out evenly. Bake at 350 degrees for 35 minutes or until almonds are golden brown. Cool and cut into a dozen bars. Wrap in aluminum foil.

CEREAL BAR

3 cups dry CEREAL (oatmeal, barley, wheat germ, wheat or corn flakes, etc.)
2½ cups POWDERED MILK
1 cup GRANULATED SUGAR (white or brown)
½ package citrus-flavored GELATIN (Jello or similar)
3 tablespoons HONEY
¼ teaspoon SALT
3 tablespoons WATER

Place all ingredients (except gelatin) in a mixing bowl and mix well. Combine the water and honey and bring to a boil. Dissolve the gelatin in the honey-water mixture. Add dry ingredients and mix well. Add additional water a teaspoonful at a time until the mixture is soft enough to mold. Make into blocks about 2 x 2 x 1 1/2 inches. Makes five blocks. Each block provides approximately 400 calories and will keep indefinitely.

BASIC TRAIL FOOD

3 cups OATMEAL or WHEAT
3 tablespoons HONEY
½ package flavored GELATIN
2½ cups powdered MILK
1 cup white or brown SUGAR

Mix all dry ingredients except gelatin. Add 3 tablespoons water to honey and bring to a boil. Dissolve gelatin in honey mixture. Add mixture to dry ingredients in large bowl. After mixing, add water, a teaspoon at a time, until the mixture is moist enough to mold. Pack in refrigerator dish.

(For taste variations: add dried apricots, raisins, dates, or peanut butter. May be molded and shaped onto aluminum foil. May be frozen.)

BARS OF IRON

1/3 cup BUTTER or
   MARGARINE
1 cup dark RAISINS
½ cup golden RAISINS
½ cup SUGAR
½ cup golden MOLASSES
1 EGG
1¼ cup whole wheat FLOUR
¼ cup nonfat DRY MILK
¼ cup toasted WHEAT GERM
1½ teaspoon BAKING POWDER
½ teaspoon BAKING SODA
1 cup sliced ALMONDS
½ cup LIQUID MILK
1 cup quick-cooking
   rolled OATS
½ teaspoon SALT
½ teaspoon GINGER

Chop raisins. Cream butter, sugar, and molasses together. Combine whole wheat flour, non-fat dry milk, wheat germ, baking powder, soda, salt and ginger and mix lightly. Blend into creamed mixture alternately with liquid milk. Stir in oats, raisins, and half of the almonds. Turn into greased baking pan (9 x 12) and spread evenly. Sprinkle with remaining half cup of almonds. Bake in moderate oven (350 F) about 30 minutes until cookies test done. Cool in pan, then cut into bars. (Makes 24 bars, 2 x 2 inches.)

HIKERS BIRD SEED

12 to 16 ounces CHOCOLATE CHIPS or M&M's (depending on temperature)

8 ounces unsalted NUTS (peanuts, sunflower seeds, etc. and/or combinations)

8 ounces DRIED FRUIT (raisins, currants, chopped dates, etc. and/or combinations)

2 cups DRY CEREAL (Rice Krispies, Trix, etc., not flakes)

Mix well and put one cupful in a plastic bag. This is an old standby that shows up on almost every hike in one form or another.

PEMMICAN

This was originally a cold climate trail food which was very high in fat (suet). The recipe which follows substitutes honey instead of suet for a binder. However, suet can be substituted for a cold weather trip.

2 cups RAISINS

2 cups dry DATES

Enough HONEY for a binder

2 cups NUTS (peanuts, cashews, walnuts, etc.) or 1 cup of your favorite dry cereal

Grind together all ingredients except honey. Add honey a little at a time, mixing well until moist enough to mold well and hold shape. Pour into a pan until about 3/4 inch thick, or mold directly into bars. Refrigerate and cut off bars from the pan and wrap in aluminum foil.

PEANUT BAR

½ cup PEANUT BUTTER (chunky)

½ cup HONEY

½ cup DRY MILK POWDER

Heat peanut butter in a double boiler until it is a thick soup. Stir in the honey and then the dry milk. Mix well and remove from heat. Pack into cupcake papers.

#1: Refrigerate bars, then coat with semi-sweet or dipping chocolate.

#2: Mix shredded coconut in the chocolate before dipping.

(Makes 6 quarter-cup bars or 3 half-cup bars.)

WHEELS OF STEEL

½ cup BUTTER or Margarine
½ cup PEANUT BUTTER
1 cup RAISINS
1 cup BROWN SUGAR (packed)
1 EGG

¼ cup toasted WHEAT GERM
¾ cup WHOLE WHEAT FLOUR
1 teaspoon VANILLA
½ cup nonfat DRY MILK
¾ teaspoon SALT

1 cup quick-cooking ROLLED OATS
¼ teaspoon BAKING POWDER
¼ teaspoon SODA
3 tablespoons LIQUID MILK
sesame seeds (optional)

Chop raisins. Cream butter, peanut butter, sugar, egg and vanilla well. Combine whole wheat flour, wheat germ, nonfat dry milk, salt, baking powder and soda and stir together lightly. Stir into creamed mixture. Add liquid milk, oats and raisins and mix well. For each cookie, place a heaping teaspoon of the dough on a greased baking sheet and spread to a four-inch circle. Sprinkle with about one teaspoon sesame seeds. Bake for 15 minutes in a 350 oven. Remove from oven and allow cookies to stand about five minutes on baking sheet. Remove to a wire rack to cool. (Bake only four cookies to a large baking sheet, to prevent running together. Because of the large size, these cookies are fragile while hot.)

SIERRA COOKIES

1. Combine the following in a large bowl, then mix at medium speed:

1 cup SHORTENING
2 tablespoons VANILLA
1 teaspoon CINNAMON
2/3 cup MILK
1 cup BROWN SUGAR (packed)
2 teaspoons NUTMEG
2 EGGS

2. Then add following and mix at slow speed:

2 cups FLOUR
1 teaspoon SALT
1 teaspoon SODA

3. Clean off batters and hand-mix the following:

½ jar GLAZED FRUIT
½ package sliced WALNUTS
½ box RAISINS

4. Mix thoroughly, then blend in by hand 4 cups of OATMEAL. Press down in a greased 12 x 18 inch cookie pan with the back of a wet spoon. Bake in a 350 degree oven for 20 minutes. Cut into 24 pieces and wrap in aluminum foil or put in plastic bags. (If they're not to be eaten within a few weeks, keep in freezer to prevent mold from forming.)

QUICK ENERGY COOKIES

1 cup RAISINS
2/3 cup DRIED FRUIT
1/3 cup COCONUT
½ cup non-fat DRY MILK
¼ teaspoon BAKING POWDER
¾ teaspoon SALT
¼ teaspoon BAKING SODA
¾ cup WHOLE WHEAT FLOUR
½ cup GRANOLA

1/3 cup WHEAT GERM
½ cup BUTTER
½ cup PEANUT BUTTER
1 cup BROWN SUGAR
2 EGGS
2 teaspoons VANILLA
5 tablespoons MILK (fresh)
½ cup SUNFLOWER SEEDS
  (raw)
1 cup ROLLED OATS
  (long-cooking)

Cut up dried fruits and raisins and hold aside. Sift dry milk, baking powder, salt and soda, and mix together. Stir in flour, wheat germ, and coconut. Cream butter thoroughly. Cream in peanut butter. Continue creaming and add brown sugar. Add eggs, beating well. Add vanilla and mix well. Alternately add flour mixture with liquid milk. Stir in sunflower seeds and remaining dry ingredients. Add cut up fruit until thoroughly distributed. Drop by tablespoonfulls on ungreased cookie sheet and permit spreading room. Bake at 375 for 10-12 minutes. (Allow cookies to dry out on cookie sheet before transferring.)

CRUNCHY CEREAL

6 cups OATMEAL
2/3 cup SUNFLOWER SEED
2/3 cup SESAME SEED
2/3 cup COCONUT
2/3 cup WHEAT GERM
½ cup LECITHIN Granules
2 teaspoons SALT

2/3 cup CHOPPED NUTS
2/3 cup DRY MILK
2 teaspoons VANILLA
2/3 cup CORN SYRUP
¼ cup WATER
2/3 cup OIL

Put the dry ingredients into a large roaster pan. Mix vanilla with corn syrup. Add 1/4 cup water. Mix and add vegetable oil. Add liquids to dry ingredients and mix well. Bake 30 minutes at 250 degrees. Turn with pancake turner and continue baking until golden (about 15-20 minutes). Cool and add raisins and cut dates if desired.

BEEF JERKY #1

Cut beef or venison in foot-long strips. Must be cut with grain for stringiness. Make a strong salt and water solution. Dip meat strips into brine until meat is white. Lay strips in the sun . Meat must hang until thoroughly dry. Store strips in container with holes in cover, or use cloth sacks to allow air to penetrate to meat. Meat can be eaten as jerky or simmered in stew pot.

BEEF JERKY #2

Cut round steak into thin strips. Cut with the grain. Dip strips in hot brine (1/4 cup salt to a gallon water). Dip only until meat is no longer red. Drain well. Have ready a mixture of salt and coarse ground black pepper. Coat meat well on both sides. Hang meat strips from tree limbs or place on clean wire screen elevated from the ground.

The sun and air must reach the meat for drying process. Strips may be covered with a single layer of cheese cloth. Turn strips after a day or two to thoroughly dry them.

BEEF JERKY #3

1 beef FLANK STEAK
½ cup SOY SAUCE
½ teaspoon GARLIC SALT
½ teaspoon LEMON PEPPER

Trim fat from flank steak. Cut with grain into strips 1/8 inch thick. Toss with soy sauce and garlic salt and lemon pepper. Place strips close together, but not overlapping, in single layer on rack over baking sheet. Bake in a slow oven (150 to 175) overnight for 10-12 hours. Store at room temperature in air-tight containers.

(Note: Beef jerky should not be crisp. If it is, oven temperature is too high.)

SAMPLE TRAIL LUNCH CHEESE, SALAMI, JERKY
RYP CRISP, CRACKERS, MELBA TOAST
    or HARD TACK
Any DRIED FRUIT
CHOCOLATE BAR, NUTS, COOKIES

Camp Cookery

Camp cookery can range from the simple opening of cans to a full-time hobby. The following recipes are designed to keep the campers happy and the cook content.

SKILLET BREAD

    4 cups FLOUR
    2 tablespoons BAKING POWDER
    1½ teaspoons SALT
    1 teaspoon CREAM of TARTAR
    2 tablespoons SUGAR
    ¾ cup POWDERED MILK
    1 cup VEGETABLE SHORTENING
    1 teaspoon CINNAMON (optional)

Cut in shortening until the consistency of fine meal. (Mix can be stored in cool place for several weeks.) Add water to make a thick dough.

Lightly grease a frying pan. Pat out dough to an inch thickness. Fry 8 to 10 minutes on each side over low heat.

(This same mix can be used for pancakes by adding one egg per cup mix and varying the amounts of water.)

BEEF & VEGETABLE STEW

    1½ pounds STEWING BEEF   1 can WHOLE POTATOES
    ¼ cup FLOUR   2 cans TOMATO SAUCE
    1/3 cup COOKING OIL   ½ teaspoon THYME (optional)
    1 can DICED CARROTS   SALT and PEPPER
    1 can GREEN BEANS

Coat beef with flour, salt and pepper and brown in oil. Drain fat. Save liquid from carrots, beans, and potatoes. Add enough water to make 2-3 cups liquid. Add to meat. Add tomato sauce and thyme. Cover and simmer 2 hours. Add canned vegetables and heat 10 minutes longer. (Serves 5)

EASY-DO PANCAKES

1 cup Bisquick
3 tablespoons POWDERED MILK or CREAM
1 EGG

Mix Bisquick, powdered milk or cream, egg and water until the consistency is that of thick cream. (Use Teflon-coated grill or frypan to avoid greasing). Use one tablespoon of batter for each pancake. Serve with bacon or sausage.

FOIL STEW

(Ingredients per serving)
2 thick patties GROUND BEEF
1 POTATO (thinly-sliced)
1 CARROT (finely chopped)
1 ONION (thinly-sliced)
SALT and PEPPER

Place meat patties on heavy duty broiling foil. Add thinly sliced raw potato. Then add carrot slices, onion slices, salt and pepper to taste.

Fold foil around food and fold edges together to lock lengthwise and on ends. Let fire burn down until there is no flame. On a grill, cook the foil package with MEAT SIDE DOWN (about 15 to 20 minutes). Using hot gloves, flip package over, so SEAM SIDE IS DOWN. Cook 10-15 minutes more. Serve by opening foil pack and using pack as plate.

If cooking directly on coals, double wrap packs and turn frequently to avoid burning (about 20 minutes total cooking time).

DUTCH OVEN PEACH COBBLER

1 large can SLICED PEACHES
1 box YELLOW CAKE MIX
2 tablespoons SPICE MIXTURE (to include
    CINNAMON, NUTMEG, SUGAR and FLOUR)

Pour peaches (including juice) into Dutch oven. Sprinkle spice mixture over peaches. Pour cake mix over peaches and mixture. Cook about 15 minutes in hot coals. (Be sure to put coals on top of Dutch oven so top of cake will bake.)

SOME-MORES

Make a sandwich of two graham crackers and a piece of chocolate. Toast a marshmallow and either top the sandwich, or pop it into the sandwich.

DUTCH OVEN BISCUITS

Preheat Dutch oven in coals. To prevent the pan containing the biscuits from touching the bottom of the Dutch oven, put three small flat rocks on the oven bottom.

To test for oven heat, place a few drops of water on bottom of oven. The oven and the lid must be quite hot for proper baking. When the biscuit dough is ready, it should be placed in a pan in the heated oven. The oven should then be placed over a small amount of coals, and the lid covered with coals and hot ashes.

> 2 cups Bisquick
> ½ cup cold WATER

Mix ingredients with a fork until dough is of a soft consistency. Spoon dough into cake pan by spoonfuls. Bake about 10 minutes. (Makes 10 biscuits)

ONE-POT DINNER

> 1 pound HAMBURGER, mixed with one chopped ONION and rolled into small meat balls
> 4 POTATOES, sliced as for scalloped potatoes
> 4 ONIONS, quartered
> 4 stalks of CELERY, sliced
> 1 can MUSHROOM or ONION SOUP, mixed with 1/3 can WATER

Brown prepared meatballs in pot or skillet. Toss in vegetables. Add soup. Mix all ingredients together. Simmer until potatoes are done. (Serves four).

HOBO STEW

> 2 POTATOES
> 2 CARROTS
> ¼ head CABBAGE
> 3 sticks of CELERY
> 1 small can TOMATOES
> 2 BEEF BOUILLON cubes
> 1 pound GROUND BEEF
> SALT and PEPPER to taste

Cut vegetables into small pieces and break up ground beef. Put bouillon cubes in two inches of water. Simmer together with vegetables and beef for one hour in two pound coffee can. (Serves 3).

CAMPERS' STEW

4 small whole WHITE ONIONS
4 CARROTS, thinly sliced
4 POTATOES, cut into bite sized chunks
1 pound STEW MEAT, cut in bite size pieces
SALT, PEPPER, GARLIC SALT, CELERY SALT
1 package BEEF GRAVY MIX (mix with one cup
of WATER)

Divide vegetables and meat into four servings. Place on individual pieces of foil. Season to taste. Pour 1/4 cup gravy over each serving. Fold foil over as when wrapping for freezing, and turn a double seam. Cook over coals about half an hour, turning once or twice. (Serves four)

FRESH FISH BAKE

1 TROUT, or whatever the fisherman caught for
each person
1 LEMON, sliced
1 ONION, sliced

Place a slice of onion, lemon and butter in the body cavity of each fish. Salt and pepper. Fold tightly in foil and cook over coals, about ten minutes on each side (longer cooking time for larger fish).

SCONES

This hot bread can be baked on a flat surface over an open fire. Scones should be lightly browned on the outside, but thoroughly cooked on the inside.

2 cups all-purpose FLOUR   ¼ cup BUTTER
1 tablespoon SUGAR   1/3 cup MILK
1 tablespoon BAKING POWDER   2 EGGS
½ teaspoon SALT

Sift flour. Then sift again with sugar, baking powder, and salt. Cut butter into dry ingredients. Beat the milk and eggs together. Stir into dry ingredients and blend thoroughly. Turn out on a floured board and knead half a dozen times. Roll dough out to 1/2-inch thickness. Cut into 2-inch rounds. Preheat frying pan but do not grease. Place scones on pan surface and heat for ten minutes. Turn and heat for another ten minutes.

MUSHROOMS ON THE COALS

12 to 15 large fresh MUSHROOMS
4 tablespoons BUTTER, melted
¼ teaspoon GARLIC POWDER
2 tablespoons LEMON JUICE

Clean mushrooms. Cut caps in spiral design. Place in a double thickness of aluminum foil. Add butter, garlic powder and lemon juice. Seal and cook over hot coals 12-15 minutes, or until desired degree of doneness is reached.

FOIL BAKED POTATO

Scrub the potatoes before you leave home. Slice potato in half lengthwise. Take a slice of onion and a small chunk of butter and put potato back together with onion and butter in the middle. Wrap tightly in foil and bake on coals. Bake approximately 30 to 40 minutes. Turn often.

CHEESY FRANKS IN FOIL

2 cups shredded CHEDDAR CHEESE
¼ cup CHILI SAUCE
¼ cup sweet pickle RELISH
1/8 teaspoon OREGANO
8 FRANKFURTERS
8 Frankfurter BUNS

In a bowl, combine cheese, chili sauce, relish and oregano. Slit frankfurters lengthwise, but do not cut through. Place about 3 tablespoons cheese mixture in each. Place frankfurters in buns and set each on a double thick rectangle of aluminum foil. Fold foil down onto sandwich in tight double fold. Twist ends. Place on grill folded side down for 10 minutes. Turn and heat 10 additional minutes.

CAMPFIRE FONDUE

2 cups (8 ounces) shredded Cheddar or Swiss CHEESE
2 tablespoons all-purpose FLOUR
¼ teaspoon PAPRIKA
1 can (10½ ounces) condensed CREAM OF CELERY SOUP
½ cup BEER, WHITE WINE or WATER

Toss together cheese, flour and paprika. Combine soup and beer. Heat. Over low heat add cheese, stirring until completely melted. Serve with French bread cubes.

Ember Cooking

Ember cooking refers to the direct baking of such vegetables as potatoes, corn, and squash right on charcoal briquets.

To start the charcoal fire, stack the briquets in a pyramid. This will create a draft and the coals will light faster. To use a liquid starter, spray the coals and let the liquid penetrate for a few minutes before lighting. Or, simply use the self-starting briquets.

(NOTE: Do NOT use flammable liquids like gasoline or kerosene when starting up a briquet fire.)

Allow the coals to burn for about half an hour before adding the vegetables. Use kitchen tongs to spread the coals out in a single layer. Then, place the vegetables right on top of the coals. Turn the vegetables frequently.

(NOTE: The briquet coals are ready for grilling when they are covered with a gray ash during the day, or are burning fiery red at night.)

EMBER ROASTED POTATOES

Place white baking potatoes in hot coals, leaving a few coals to surround each. Turn frequently with tongs until fork tender (about 1 1/2 hours).

When cooked, remove from coals and serve immediately with butter, salt and pepper.

EMBER ROASTED SQUASH

Place butternut or acorn squash in hot coals, leaving a few coals to surround each. Turn frequently with tongs until fork tender, about 1 1/2 hours. When cooked, remove from coals. Cut in half and remove seeds. Serve immediately with butter, salt, and pepper.

EMBER ROASTED CORN

Pull husks halfway down ears of corn. Remove all silk. Sprinkle the ears of corn with unsalted water. Pull husks back over the kernels and twist shut. Place corn around the edge of hot coals. Turn frequently with tongs until tender (about 20-30 minutes). Remove husks. Serve with butter, salt, and pepper.

PEPPER ROAST

1 ROUND-BONE ARM CHUCK ROAST (about 3 pounds)
Unseasoned MEAT TENDERIZER
1 cup wine VINEGAR
½ cup SALAD OIL
3 tablespoons LEMON JUICE
1 small ONION, chopped (¼ cup)
2 teaspoons OREGANO
1 BAY LEAF, crushed
¼ cup PEPPERCORNS

Moisten meat and sprinkle with meat tenderizer. Place meat in shallow glass dish. Mix together the vinegar, oil, lemon juice, onion, oregano, and bay leaf. Pour over the meat. Cover and put in refrigerator for two hours. Turn meat often in the marinade.

After two hours refrigeration, remove meat from marinade and place on cutting board. Pound half the crushed peppercorns into each side with edge of a saucer. Set meat on grill over hot coals and grill until juices appear. Turn meat and grill an additional 15-20 minutes. Remove to cutting board and slice diagonally.

DILL POTATO SALAD

4 cups sliced cooked POTATOES
1 can (1 pound) cut GREEN BEANS, drained
1/3 cup VINEGAR
1 tablespoon instant minced ONION
1 teaspoon SALT
1 teaspoon SUGAR
½ teaspoon DILL
2 hard-cooked EGGS, chopped
1 cup dairy SOUR CREAM
3 tablespoons chopped PIMIENTO (2 ounces)

In a bowl combine vinegar, onion, salt, sugar and dill. Pour over potatoes and beans. Toss to coat evenly. Cover and chill to blend flavors. Add eggs, sour cream and pimiento. Toss lightly.

BARBECUED SHRIMP

1 cup OIL
1 tablespoon BROWN SUGAR
1 tablespoon SALT
1 tablespoon DRY MUSTARD
1 tablespoon WORCESTERSHIRE SAUCE
¼ teaspoon LIQUID SMOKE
½ cup Burgundy WINE

For marinade, combine all ingredients in flat pan and mix thoroughly. Peel and split raw shrimp and marinate for half an hour. Remove shrimp and broil over charcoal fire. Serve with cocktail sauce.

BARBEQUED SHORT RIBS

5 pounds lean beef SHORT RIBS, 3-4 inches long
¼ cup SALAD OIL
¼ cup SOY SAUCE
¼ cup WINE VINEGAR
¼ cup ORANGE MARMALADE
2 tablespoons WORCHESTERSHIRE SAUCE
1 tablespoon DRIED MUSTARD
1 teaspoon dried PARSLEY flakes
1 teaspoon GARLIC SALT
½ teaspoon LEMON PEPPER

Place short ribs in large bowl. Combine remaining ingredients; pour over ribs. Cover and refrigerate 8 to 10 hours or overnight, turning occasionally. Remove from marinade and drain thoroughly. Cook slowly on grill 7 to 8 inches from coals, 1 1/2 to 2 hours or until meat begins to leave bone, turning frequently. Brush with marinade during last 20 minutes of cooking time. (Serves 6)

GARLIC BREAD

4 tablespoons BUTTER
1 teaspoon GARLIC POWDER
¼ teaspoon SALT
1 large loaf FRENCH BREAD

Blend garlic salt with softened butter. Cut French or Italian bread into thick slices ON THE BIAS. Do not cut through the bottom crust. Spread the garlic butter between slices. Wrap loaf in foil, place on grill and turn several times.

APPLE-SAUSAGE KABOBS

1 pound fresh PORK LINK SAUSAGES
¼ pound fresh whole mushrooms (or one 4-ounce can, drained)
1 large GREEN PEPPER
8 cherry TOMATOES
8 whole white ONIONS

Sauce   ¼ cup bottled CHILI SAUCE
¼ cup canned APPLE SAUCE
1 tablespoon LEMON JUICE
1 teaspoon SUGAR
¼ teaspoon CHILI POWDER

Cook sausage links in skillet until brown (about 10 minutes). Drain on paper towel. Use whole, or cut in half. Cut green pepper into one-inch square pieces. Wash fresh mushrooms and cherry tomatoes. Trim stems from mushrooms.

Thread sausage links, green pepper, mushrooms, tomatoes and onions alternately onto skewers and place on grill over hot coals. Baste with sauce. Cook 5 to 10 minutes, turning occasionally and continuing to baste with sauce.

GLAZE for RIBS

1 1/3 cups HONEY
4 tablespoons SOY SAUCE
3 drops TABASCO SAUCE
¼ teaspoon freshly ground black PEPPER

Cut spareribs into serving-sized pieces. Put spareribs in a roasting pan. Combine soy sauce, pepper, Tabasco and spread over meat. Pour on the honey. Let stand for 1/2 hour. Turn spareribs over and baste with sauce. Let stand for another 1/2 hour. Place in 350 oven and roast for about 1 1/2 hours. Turn and baste while cooking. (If crispness is desired, roast ribs on rack.)

BUTTERED CORN BARBEQUE

Remove the husks from corn. Blend herb seasoning (finely ground) with softened butter. Spread this mixture over each ear of corn. Wrap tightly in heavy duty aluminum foil. Bake over hot coals for 15-20 minutes, turning several times.

ZESTY BAR-B-Q SAUCE

1 cup CATSUP
1¼ cups WATER
¼ cup BROWN SUGAR
¼ cup VINEGAR
2 tablespoons WORCESTERSHIRE SAUCE
1 teaspoon CELERY SALT
1 teaspoon CHILI POWDER
¼ teaspoon PEPPER
2 tablespoons FLOUR

Combine all ingredients in a saucepan and cook over low heat about 10 minutes. Stir occasionally. Serve over meat or rice. (Makes about 2 cups)

BARBECUED RIBS

3 - 4 pounds RIBS (PORK or VENISON)
1 tablespoon SALT
2 tablespoons PICKLING SPICES
1 tablespoon BROWN SUGAR

Cover ribs with water. Add above ingredients. Bring to slow boil and cook 1 1/2 hours or until tender. Cool. Prepare barbecue sauce.

BARBECUE SAUCE
1 medium ONION chopped and browned in butter
¾ cup hot BARBECUE SAUCE
¼ cup light CORN SYRUP

Bake ribs 1/2 hour, basting with sauce. Then, broil about 5 minutes on each side and serve.
(These ribs can also be made on an outdoor grill instead of baking in the oven. Turn ribs often on the grill, basting each time. Takes about an hour.)

BROILED SIRLOIN STEAK

1 or 2 BEEF SIRLOIN STEAKS, cut 1 to 2 inches thick
SALT and PEPPER

Place steaks on grill. For one-inch steaks, set grill about 2 to 3 inches from heat. For two-inch steaks, set grill 3 to 5 inches from heat.
When one side is browned, turn the steaks, season with salt and pepper and finish cooking the second side. (Allow 20 minutes TOTAL cooking time for rare, and about 25-30 minutes for medium.)

CHUCKWAGON CHUCK STEAKS

2 BEEF BLADE STEAKS, cut ½ to ¾ inch thick
1 medium-sized ONION, chopped
1 cup CATSUP
1/3 cup VINEGAR
2 tablespoons BROWN SUGAR

2 teaspoons SALT
1 clove GARLIC, crushed
1 BAY LEAF
1/8 teaspoon HOT PEPPER
SAUCE

Combine onion, catsup, vinegar, brown sugar, salt, garlic, bay leaf and hot sauce in saucepan and cook slowly 10 minutes, stirring occasionally. Cool. Pour sauce over steaks in a glass dish, turning to coat all sides. Marinate in refrigerator overnight. Pour off and reserve marinade.

Place steaks on grill and broil for 20-25 minutes. Turn and brush steaks with sauce occasionally. (This recipe should be doubled to serve four.)

B-B-Q SAUCE

1¼ pounds fresh
MARROW BONES
1 pint WATER
1¼ quarts canned TOMATOES
1 stem GARLIC, chopped
1 BAY LEAF
1 teaspoon CELERY SEED
1 tablespoon SALT
1 teaspoon SUGAR

3 CLOVES
½ GREEN PEPPER
1 sliced ONION
¼ bottle WORCESTERSHIRE
SAUCE
¾ cups VINEGAR
1 tablespoon grated
HORSERADISH
2 dashes TABASCO SAUCE

Wash marrow bones and discard excess fat. Mix all ingredients EXCEPT the Worcestershire sauce, vinegar, horseradish, and Tabasco sauce. Simmer for four hours. Chill and let stand overnight in the refrigerator.

Heat sauce, remove and discard the bones. Press all the pulp possible through a fine strainer. Add the last four ingredients. Taste and add more seasoning, if desired. (Makes one quart). Serve hot.

GRILLED LAMB RIB CHOPS

Chops should be from 1 to 11/2 inches thick. Cover bone ends with aluminum foil to prevent charring. Rub grill with lamb fat, and set chops on grill. Cook ten minutes on each side. To determine degree of doneness, make a tiny slit next to the bone. A slightly pinkish color is preferred. Serve at once.

SPARERIBS IN SAUCE

3 pounds lean SPARERIBS

Marinade

¼ cup SOY SAUCE
1/3 cup CORN SYRUP
1/3 cup LEMON JUICE
1 clove GARLIC, crushed

½ teaspoon DRY MUSTARD
¼ teaspoon ground CLOVES
¼ teaspoon TABASCO SAUCE
¼ teaspoon SALT

Trim fat from spareribs, but do not separate. Blend marinade ingredients. Put ribs on heavy duty aluminum wrap large enough to cover ribs completely. Turn the foil up around the ribs and pour marinade over ribs. Double-close foil across for 2 to 2 1/2 hours. Put foil-wrapped ribs on grill about six inches above hot grey coals. Cook for an hour, turning occasionally. Open foil, and cut into serving pieces.

GRILLED SPARERIBS

Lay raw ribs on a grill about six inches above glowing coals. Grill very slowly, turning often. Allow at least an hour for grilling. Brush with sauce after grilling and serve.

SPARERIB SEASONING

6 tablespoons SALT
6 tablespoons SUGAR
1 tablespoon DRY LEMON POWDER
2 tablespoons SAVOR SALT
2½ tablespoons black PEPPER
1 tablespoon PAPRIKA

This is a dry rib seasoning which can be used for sprinkling on spareribs prior to barbecuing.

PIQUANT BARBEQUE SAUCE

1 teaspoon CORNSTARCH
¼ teaspoon DRY MUSTARD
¼ cup cider VINEGAR
1 cup tomato CATSUP

¼ cup BROWN SUGAR
½ teaspoon ONION SALT
½ teaspoon CELERY SALT
SALT and PEPPER

Dissolve the cornstarch and mustard in vinegar. Add the remaining ingredients. Cook, stirring constantly, until thickened. (This sauce is good with chicken, hamburgers, or spareribs.)

ROASTED ONIONS

Select good-sized Bermuda onions. Do not peel. Prick through with a long-tined fork several times. (This prevents bursting when cooking.) Place each onion on a square of heavy duty aluminum foil and wrap securely. Place on grill and cook, rolling around and turning several times. When soft, open and turn back foil. Slit with a sharp knife (as if for a potato). Add butter, salt, and pepper.

SUMMER SQUASH

2 pounds ZUCCHINI, sliced
2 TOMATOES, peeled and chopped
1 ONION, thinly sliced
1½ teaspoons SALT
½ teaspoon PEPPER
½ teaspoon dried or 3 sprigs fresh BASIL
½ teaspoon OREGANO
3 tablespoons BUTTER

Place zucchini, tomatoes and onion in center of large square of heavy duty aluminum foil. Sprinkle with salt, pepper, basil and oregano. Dot with butter. Bring foil up over vegetables and seal with a fold to make a tight package. Cook on grill over a medium fire, shaking occasionally, about 30-40 minutes.

WESTERN KABOBS

2 pounds boneless STEAK
½ cup SOY SAUCE
½ teaspoon GINGER
2 tablespoons SALAD OIL
1 tablespoon SUGAR
1 cup PINEAPPLE chunks, drained, or fresh pineapple
1 basket CHERRY TOMATOES

Cut meat into 1" cubes. Pierce meat with fork so marinade can penetrate. Combine soy sauce, ginger, salad oil and sugar. Pour over meat cubes. Allow to stand for at least 1 hour. Turn occasionally.

Put meat on skewers, leaving space between pieces. Put pineapple chunks and tomatoes on other skewers. Broil meat over hot coals. When meat is turned, add skewers of pineapple and tomatoes to the grill. Brush skewers of food with marinade.

PATIO POTATO SALAD

1/3 cup ITALIAN DRESSING
1 teaspoon instant minced ONIONS
1 teaspoon SALT
4 cups cubed cooked POTATOES (about 1½ pounds)
1½ cups COTTAGE CHEESE
¾ cup chopped CELERY
1 hard-cooked EGG, chopped
TOMATO wedges

Combine dressing, onion and salt. Add to potatoes and toss lightly. Cover and chill to blend flavors. Add cottage cheese, celery and egg. Toss lightly. Garnish with tomato wedges.

MARINATED FLANK STEAK

1 BEEF FLANK STEAK (1¼ to 1¾ pounds)

Marinade
¼ cup SALAD OIL
1 tablespoon LEMON JUICE
1 clove GARLIC, crushed
½ teaspoon SALT
¼ teaspoon PEPPER

Combine salad oil, lemon juice, garlic, salt and pepper. Place steak in flat glass dish and pour marinade over it. Cover pan with foil and refrigerate overnight, turning occasionally. Pour off and reserve marinade.

Place steak on grill and broil for 5-8 minutes. Turn, brush with marinade and broil an additional 5 minutes or to desired doneness. Slice diagonally across grain in thin strips. (Serves 4).

ROAST ON THE ROCKS

Meat should be at room temperature. Rub roast with salt, coarse black pepper, and garlic salt. place the meat directly on the coals in an outdoor grill. (For rare roast, allow 15-20 minutes' roasting time per pound; for medium, 20-25 minutes.)

Cook on coals (turning occasionally) until all sides have a charred coating. Place on wooden cutting board and slice thickly. The meat juice will ooze out during carving, and should be served over the meat slices.

HAMBURGER MIX

1 pound GROUND BEEF
½ teaspoon SALT
¼ teaspoon PEPPER
1 tablespoon chopped ONION
1/8 teaspoon GARLIC SALT

Mix ground beef with salt, pepper, chopped onion, and garlic salt. Shape into patties. Cook on grill, turning once.

CHILI-CHEESE BURGERS

1 cup grated CHEESE
¼ cup MILK
½ tablespoon CHILI POWDER

To basic recipe, add above ingredients and cook on grill.

MUSTARD BURGERS

To basic recipe, add one-half teaspoon dry mustard and cook on grill.

ONIONBURGERS

3 pounds GROUND BEEF
1 package (1 3/8 ounces) ONION SOUP MIX
2/3 cup WATER

Combine onion soup mix with water and add to ground beef. Stir lightly and shape into patties, about 1/2 inch thick. Place on grill about 15 minutes, turning once. (Serves 8)

BUTTER BARBECUE SAUCE

½ cup (1 stick) BUTTER
½ cup chopped ONION
½ cup CATSUP
¼ cup firmly packed light BROWN SUGAR
3 tablespoons WORCESTERSHIRE SAUCE

1½ teaspoons CHILI POWDER
1 teaspoon SALT
1/8 teaspoon PEPPER

In a saucepan, melt butter. Add onion and saute until tender. Stir in catsup, sugar, Worcestershire sauce, chili powder, salt, and pepper. Simmer for 5 minutes. Use this sauce to baste hamburger patties while grilling. (Sauce stores well in refrigerator, but should be warmed before using.)

Notes

Index

Salsa Lovers Cook Book

More than 180 recipes for salsa, dips, salads, appetizers and more!

$9.95

Quick-n-Easy Mexican Recipes

Make your favorite Mexican dishes in record time! Excellent tacos, tostadas, enchiladas and more!

$9.95

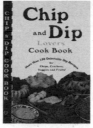

Chip and Dip Lovers Cook Book

Easy and colorful recipes from Southwestern salsas to quick appetizer dips!

$9.95

Tortilla Lovers' Cook Book

Celebrate the tortilla with more than 100 easy recipes for breakfast, lunch, dinner, appetizers and desserts, too!

$9.95

Chili Lovers Cook Book

Prize-winning recipes for chili, with or without beans. Plus a variety of taste-tempting foods made with flavorful chile peppers.

$9.95

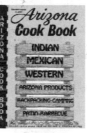

Arizona Cook Book

A collection of authentic Arizona recipes. Including Indian, Mexican and Western foods.

$9.95

New Mexico Cook Book

This unique book explores the age-old recipes that are rich with the heritage of New Mexico.

$9.95

Easy RV Recipes

Easy recipes for the traveling cook. Over 200 recipes to make in your RV, camper or houseboat.

$9.95

Easy Recipes for Wild Game

More than 200 "wild" recipes for large and small game, wild fowl and fish.

$9.95

Apple Lovers Cook Book

What's more American than eating apple pie? Try these 150 favorite recipes for appetizers, main and side dishes, muffins, pies, salads, beverages and preserves.

$9.95

Pumpkin Lovers Cook Book

More than 175 recipes for soups, breads, muffins, pies, cakes, cheesecakes, cookies and even ice cream! Carving tips, trivia and more.

$9.95

Mexican Family Favorites Recipes

250 authentic, home-style recipes for tacos, tamales, menudo, enchiladas, burros, salsas, frijoles, chile rellenos, carne seca, guacamole, and more!

$9.95

QTY	TITLE	PRICE	TOTAL
	Burrito Lovers' Cook Book	9.95	
	Chili Lovers' Cook Book	9.95	
	Chip & Dip Lovers' Cook Book	9.95	
	Citrus Lovers' Cook Book	9.95	
	Easy BBQ Recipes	9.95	
	Easy BBQ Sauces	9.95	
	Grand Canyon Cook Book	9.95	
	Low Fat Mexican Recipes	9.95	
	New Mexico Cook Book	9.95	
	Mexican Family Favorites Cook Book	9.95	
	Quick-n-Easy Mexican Recipes	9.95	
	Salsa Lovers' Cook Book	9.95	
	Sedona Cook Book	9.95	
	Tequila Cook Book	9.95	
	Texas Cook Book	9.95	
	Tortilla Lovers' Cook Book	9.95	
	Veggie Lovers' Cook Book	9.95	
	Western Breakfast	9.95	

US Shipping & Handling Add	1-3 Books: 5.00	
[for non-domestic ship rates, please call]	4-9 Books: 7.00	
	9+ Books: 7.00 + 0.25 per book	
	AZ residents add 8.1% sales tax	
	(US funds only) Total:	

Please make checks payable to:
Golden West Publishers
4113 N. Longview,
Phoenix, AZ 85014

☐ Check or money order enclosed
☐ MC ☐ VISA ☐ Discover ☐ American Express Verification Code:_____

Card Number:_____ Exp._____

Signature: _____

Name_____Phone:_____

Address _____

City_____State_____ZIP _____

Email _____

Prices are subject to change.

Visit our website or call us toll free for a free catalog of all our titles!